ROADSIDE BOMBS AND DEMOCRACY

BY WILLIAM LITTLE

ROADSIDE BOMBS AND DEMOCRACY

AN AMERICAN POLICE OFFICER IN IRAQ

TATE PUBLISHING & *Enterprises*

Published by Tate Publishing & Enterprises, LLC
127 E. Trade Center Terrace | Mustang, Oklahoma 73064 USA
1.888.361.9473 | www.tatepublishing.com

Tate Publishing is committed to excellence in the publishing industry. The company reflects the philosophy established by the founders, based on Psalm 68:11,
"The Lord gave the word and great was the company of those who published it."

Book design copyright © 2009 by Tate Publishing, LLC. All rights reserved.
Cover design by Stephanie Woloszyn
Interior design by Janae J. Glass

Published in the United States of America

ISBN: 978-1-60604-826-9
1. Political Science: Political Freedom & Security: Law Enforcement

09.03.09

TABLE OF CONTENTS

7/2/09

Brian,

Thank you for your service
in the "Big Sandbox". Thank
you for your interest and
support. I hope you
enjoy my book.

Thank you and
God bless,

Ron Linde

INTRODUCTION

KOSOVO

This is the story of my experiences as an international police advisor from November 2003 to December 2006. Prior to these missions, I served in the military and was a deputy sheriff. It was nothing I would consider particularly glamorous or spectacular, however. I'm not a scholar, foreign diplomat, or an expert on Middle Eastern affairs either. These are just the experiences of an ordinary guy that worked in circumstances that were on occasion extraordinary. My first overseas tour was in Kosovo from November 2003 to August 2004 with the United Nations. I also completed two tours in Iraq. My first stint was from August 2004 to August 2005; my second was from March to December 2006.

There has been a good deal of negative press, and most people view contractors in Iraq and Afghanistan as mercenaries or soldiers-for-hire. Some of this publicity may or may not be warranted. Being as my experiences as a Military Policeman in the army and as a patrol deputy for eight years were pretty low key, I definitely wouldn't consider myself a "merc" (mercenary) and I surely wouldn't qualify as one. I have a lot of respect though for the former Seals, Green Berets, et cetera that are working as contractors doing some very dangerous and necessary work in those countries.

I was never a "high speed, low drag" kind of guy. I was never in any shootouts as a cop or any firefights as a soldier. So my background was pretty mundane up to that time. In all honesty, the money offered for overseas work is very attractive, and a lot of people criticize the pay contractors make, but how else are you going to get civilians to go to a war zone and work? They say it's unfair to the servicemen and women. I whole-heartedly agree that our military should be paid much more. But why shouldn't a civilian be able to capitalize on his or her expertise? Most cops could never make that kind of money stateside. On the other side of that coin, why shouldn't someone take his military expertise into the civilian job market and be paid well for their skills? Most see it as an opportunity to better themselves and make a better future for their families. The problem is getting out of a place like Iraq in one piece, or at least alive, to enjoy it. I say to those people, "Go to Baghdad, and get a little taste for yourself. After a couple of rocket attacks and 130 degree summers in body armor, I think you'd change your tune. If you have nothing to offer to the situation or are not willing, don't criticize those who do and are willing to risk life and limb."

But the interest and motivation goes beyond the money. At least it did for me. I think most guys that are solely motivated by money will rethink it after their first IED (Improvised Explosive Device) or mortar attack. Most of the guys I met and worked with were not just motivated by the money. I'd have to say it was a combination of the adventure, danger, and the desire to do a difficult job and do it well. A lot of former cops are probably adrenaline junkies and need that type of environment to feel alive and useful. Most officers had a sincere desire to be a part of something important and to make a difference in the world. But believe me, most guys wouldn't go to a place like Iraq for $30 or $40,000 a year. Myself included. Although in all fairness, I actually met some that would.

So what would drive or motivate this particular forty-something guy, married twenty-plus years, father of two, and a granddad, to go to work in a country where soldiers are being killed almost daily by IED'S, mortars, etc? I guess it all started after the First Gulf War. I served as an MP in an Army Reserve unit processing EPW'S (Enemy Prisoners of War) in Saudi Arabia for about six months. It wasn't very exciting and not what I had envisioned when I volunteered to go.

I got out of the reserves in 1994 and went to work as a deputy in 1995. I always regretted not being able to do more in the First Gulf War. I had buddies that actually did combat operations into Iraq. I guess I was always envious. I felt like I hadn't really accomplished much. Instead of being in the "thick" of it, I felt I was "in the rear with the gear."

After being a street deputy for several years I heard some fellow officers talking about some companies that were recruiting cops to work overseas as advisors. That sounded pretty cool, and I was pretty much in a rut, but I had two kids in school and just wasn't sure I wanted to make an overseas commitment. Things started to heat up in Iraq again with sanctions, no fly zones, and military strikes.

APPLYING TO THE "COMPANY"

Finally in March 2003, Operation Iraqi Freedom kicked off. I had wanted to go to Iraq since Operation Desert Storm, and this piqued my interest. So I completed and submitted an application to see if advisors were being sent to Iraq. I won't mention the company by name because when you sign a contract with them, you are required to sign a confidentiality form. Not that I'm going to disclose any industrial secrets, but I will err on the side of caution.

The application process is quite long. They send you an application and security packet that would make Encyclopedia Britannica envious. They want to know everything to the minutest detail. Then there's the medical screening. The process is pretty thorough, and rightfully so. However, I did learn after three overseas tours a few nuts still slip through the cracks. So after this entire ordeal, I was informed they were looking for more experienced officers for Iraq, and I didn't qualify. I figured being crazy enough to want to go there was qualifier enough. But I was asked if I would be interested in going to Kosovo. I didn't really know much about it but remembered hearing on the news about the Serbs and the ethnic cleansing that had gone on in that region. So I figured it might be a worthwhile trip. It was a U.N. mission, so in many aspects it turned out to be an exercise in futility personified.

After you completed the application, and if you were accepted, you got a call with a reporting date. Again, the decision to leave and start out on this little adventure was difficult. I had been a deputy for eight years and was pretty secure in the job; I also had reservations about leaving the wife and kids, and my mother was ill. After discussing it further and getting the okay from the family, I decided to go for it. I can't say enough about my wife. She has always been very supportive. She basically told me that she knew I wouldn't be happy unless I did this, so she reassured me it was fine.

TRAINING IN VIRGINIA

The "company" has a training facility they use in the Fredericksburg, VA area. There were around seventy or eighty applicants that reported to Virginia. All cops from all over the U.S. In the building where we did most of our training there's a display of law enforcement patches put there by previous officers going on mission. When we received our first briefing, we were told that some of us would not be going because there were a limited number of slots. Well, most cops are alpha male types and competitive, so it becomes every man for himself. Not in an ugly sort of way, but there was definitely a competitive air. The training selection process ran from the 14th through the 21st. The training consisted of basic weapons training, self defense, first aid, history, and culture classes on the situation in Kosovo. We also got briefings from State Department reps on the U.N. mission and U.S. goals there. We were also issued uniforms and equipment. Our uniform while in Kosovo was a blue BDU (military style Battle Dress Uniform) with an American flag patch on the left shoulder, a U.N. patch on the right. Also a patch on the left breast pocket said U.S. CIVPOL (Civilian Police), and on your right breast pocket was your last name. We would carry a Beretta 9mm pistol and a total of three magazines. We were also issued soft body armor with no shock or trauma plate to wear under our uniform.

I'm a history buff but definitely not a history scholar. So here's a little background on Kosovo. This comes from what I read and the information discussed during training and what I learned in the country. Kosovo, which was part of the former Yugoslavia, was a tenuous combination of Serbs, Croats, and Albanians. During the early 1800s, the region was broken down as Croatia, Slavonia, Bosna, Serbia, and Montenegro. What is now Kosovo was part of the Ottoman Empire at one time. The Serbs are generally Christian and the Albanians Muslim. At the time of my mission, Kosovo was an autonomous body under U.N. protection. It is surrounded by Macedonia to the south, Albania to the southwest, Montenegro to the northwest, and Serbia to the north.

Both the Serbs and Albanians are a proud people, and their hatred runs deep for each other. The Serbs consider themselves the heroic liberators of the Slavic people. The battle of Kosovo was fought in 1389 in which the Serbs defeated the Turks. Even though the Albanians are culturally and ethnically different from the Serbs, they also take pride in the defeat of the Turks. In WWI, the Serbs fought well with the Allies against the Axis powers. After the war the Serbs had the political power, and the Croats and Slovenians had the economic power.

During WWII, the Croats fought with the Germans

in which Serbs and Gypsies were killed. Kosovo became an independent protectorate under Italy, and Serbia fell under Germany's control. When the Italians surrendered in 1943 and exited the war, the Germans took over Kosovo. Ethnic Albanians were recruited and equipped by the Germans to become S.S. troops, the Skanderbeg Division, and thousands of Serb civilians were killed, raped, robbed, etc. The murders included Serbian Priests. The Italians had tried to restrain the genocide of the Serbs where the Germans encouraged it. Marshal Tito, who was a Croat and a communist, was able to form a multi-ethnic partisan group which fought against the Germans. After WWII, Tito became the leader of "The League of Communists of Yugoslavia." Tito was able to hold the different groups together as a country. The Serbs, Croats, and Slavs were at the top of the food chain with the Albanians on the bottom.

In 1970, Tito died, and a power struggle ensued. In 1974, a new Yugoslav constitution declared Kosovo an autonomous province within Serbia, giving it more power and equality. In 1989, Slobodan Milosevic became President of Serbia. After Milosevic came to power, and since he was a Serb, he started to change things for the worse as far as Albanians were concerned. In 1989, he stripped Kosovo of its autonomy. In 1990, a Serbification program began in which thousands of Albanians were dismissed from governmental and professional jobs.

In 1991, a Kosovo government in exile was formed and independence from Serbia was declared. In 1992, Ibrahim Rugova was elected President of the so-called Kosovo Republic. Around 1994, the K.L.A., or the Kosovo Liberation

Army, was formed. This was the Albanian rebel forces which fought against the Serbian forces. Atrocities were apparently committed by both sides on some level. In 1995, the Dayton Accords ordered Milosevic to stop ethnic cleansing. In 1999, NATO finally stepped in to stop the slaughter. Serbian forces were bombed and eventually U.N. peacekeeping forces moved in to maintain the cease fire. Milosevic was eventually driven from power and arrested to be tried for war crimes. However, he died in his cell in March 2006. Okay, enough of the history lesson, but it's important to understand or try to understand the area you're going to and the people there; I also wanted to give you, the reader, some background.

Part of the selection process was a physical agility test and a psych interview. These two areas washed out several people. As I said before, a nut always slips through the crack. One guy from California ended up trashing his room, scaring the pants off his roommate, and running around the hotel where we were staying in his underwear. Needless to say, he was on the next flight back to sunny California. Yeah, you guessed it; he had passed the psych interview.

During training, I gravitated towards a couple of other officers close to my own age. It's funny how we try so hard to diversify and integrate people and force them into one group. But people will always end up into their own little cliques. It's mostly unintentional but mostly human nature. One of my new acquaintances was Mel Lankford, a good old country boy from Georgia. The second was Mark Lewis, a Starbucks junkie from Seattle, Washington. Mark and I would end up working together once we got into Kosovo.

LEAVING FOR KOSOVO

On the twentieth, we got to take a trip to D.C., and I got to see the Law Enforcement Memorial Wall for the first time. So we left Virginia on the 22nd. We flew out of Dulles International through Vienna, Austria, to our final destination, the "International" airport in Pristina, the capital of Kosovo. When we arrived, we were bussed to a little hotel several miles away. The name was the Hotel Beni. It appeared to be recently built; it was white with a steeply sloped roof, and it was very quaint looking. It had nice concrete planters, a columned gazebo, a courtyard with globed lampposts, and white wrought iron balcony rails. Looks can be deceiving, though. Mel, Mark, and I were put in a room the size of a walk-in closet. It reminded me of a *Three Stooges* movie, trying to move around or dress. It was comical. The shower was a hole in the floor with a water hose. Breakfast consisted of boiled eggs, sliced tomatoes, cucumbers, and some kind of bologna-looking meat. Since I had been in the Army and had served overseas, it wasn't a big surprise to me. For some guys who'd never been out of the states, it was real culture shock.

Fortunately, Mel had done a previous tour and knew another American officer who was working in Pristina and had an apartment. So after a couple of days of being in a room so small you had to step outside to change your mind, Mel asked Mark and I if we'd be interested. Well, needless to say, he didn't have to ask twice, and we packed up and got out of there. Mel's buddy was a retired Chicago cop who'd been in Kosovo working for several years. He was assigned to some secret squirrel investigations unit. Who knows? Maybe he's still there.

U.N. TRAINING

The apartment was a decent place which included a maid. On the twenty-fourth, we started our training at the U.N.M.I.K. (United Nations Mission in Kosovo) Police training center. This lasted about a week. Our trainers were from all over the globe: Germany, France, Russia, Italy, etc. The training consisted of mine awareness (as in land mines), officer survival, history, cultural awareness, and shooting. Now, I said before what my impression of the U.N. was. The shooting test, if I remember right, was being able to put five rounds out of about ten in a man-sized target at about ten feet. Now, as easy as that sounds, some had problems with that. The shooting test was conducted at a makeshift range outside Pristina, which consisted of a HESCO wall topped with barbed wire.

Now, the guy who invented HESCO barriers must be rich. They're a metal frame and some type of cloth or fabric container goes inside that's filled with sand or soil. They can't cost a lot to manufacture, and I'm sure they're sold for top dollar. We were told not to wander outside the range area because there was the possibility of unexploded mines in the area. Good thing we had that mine awareness training. I watched a sheep herder with a large flock move through the area. Nothing ever exploded, so either he knew where to walk or the good Lord was watching out for him. Now, last but not least, we had to take an English test. Now, the other American officers and I were thinking, *You're kidding right? We're from America; we write, read, and speak English. Now, why do you need to test us?* Well, of course there are officers from other countries who don't have a very good grasp of the language, as evidenced by the people who were actually giving the test. I almost failed because I couldn't understand the person who was administering the test! Overall the training was pretty much a joke. It lacked the depth and intensity I would have expected.

Now, Pristina was not a bad city. It had numerous high rise buildings. A lot of them were old communist-style housing projects. They were the cookie-cutter type that you might see in any former eastern bloc country. Some of the streets were littered with garbage, but overall it wasn't bad under the circumstances. You could tell it must have been a pretty modern city at one time. There was one building that had a huge mural of Bill Clinton. In fact the street was called Bill Clinton Street or Avenue. The people really seemed to love him—the Albanians anyway. The Serbs weren't too crazy about him; I'm not sure what was up with that. Hey, at least the guy had time to do one positive thing in between interns or secretaries. The "company" I worked for put on a nice little thanksgiving feast for us with all the trimmings at a hotel in Pristina. There was one club where a lot of the western officers hung out. Americans know how to live, regardless where in the world it is.

So finally about the last day or two of training officers from the different regions came to recruit us. Well, one gave a briefing about the Peja (Payuh) region and how it was the wild west of Kosovo. Peja is in the western part of Kosovo. This was the place for anyone who wanted some action. Well, I figured I'd come this far and might as well go all the way. So I broke one of the first rules I learned in the army: I volunteered.

ASSIGNMENT: PEJA

About the second of December, we were loaded onto buses and headed to our respective assignments. Mark Lewis, Jason Hinds, an officer from Texas, and I were assigned together. From Pristina to Peja, some of the countryside was nice: hilly, forested, rivers, and gorges. I can't remember the exact location, but there's a bridge that was built by the Turks right next to a modern bridge. It was made of stone and obviously centuries old. There were also signs of a war: burned and bombed out buildings, houses, and destroyed mosques.

The roads in most places were narrow and in some instances, curvy and treacherous. All of the roads were in various states of disrepair. There are numerous farms all over Kosovo. What industry that existed before the war had either been destroyed or closed due to lack of funds. However, we did pass some type of coal mine along the way that appeared to still be operational. There were also numer ous monuments along our route. I later learned that they were for either a little skirmish that had occurred or some "martyr for the cause."

Our trip took several hours and was nerve-racking, between the narrow winding roads, dodging donkey carts and "Kosovo Harleys." This is what we called a cross between a motorized tiller with handle bars and a trailer or cart. Finally, we arrived at the regional police headquarters in Peja in one piece. Once there, we had another briefing and were told who was assigned in Peja and who would move on to one of the other stations in the region.

As I look back, my first mission and real exposure to the U.N. was educational and somewhat enjoyable. At a minimum, it was an eye-opener. I met some interesting officers from all over the world. The officers from industrialized countries such as Canada, France, England, Germany, and the U.S. had a good grasp of modern police techniques. Some of the officers from countries such as Pakistan, India, and Africa were a little behind the curve as far as police techniques and technology. It's no wonder the U.N. gets so little accomplished. I seriously wonder why the U.S. pours so much money into an organization that seems to be so ineffective.

DECANI

I was assigned to a small mountain town south of Peja called Decani (Dechani). The area was scenic with an ice-cold river, the Prokletije mountain range, and a six or seven hundred-year-old Serbian monastery. The monastery was built, I believe, in the thirteenth or fourteenth century and contains numerous Byzantine paintings, Romanesque-Gothic sculptures, and icons from the fourteenth to the seventeenth century. I was able to go into the monastery on about two occasions, and the priests are somewhat secretive and protective, so I didn't get the grand tour. The only area I ever saw was the dining room; I never got to see inside, the actual sanctuary. There are about thirty villages in the area with a population of 30,000 or more. Most of the locals were farmers. The area was also deeply involved in the rebel movement which started in the 1990s against Milosevic and his regime. We were picked up at the regional HQ by two Canadian officers from our assigned station. They had been in country for several months. Their favorite term was "knob." All the locals were "knobs." We traveled in a "Coca-Cola," a red and white

U.N. vehicle that looks like a can of Coke. On the drive to Decani, we observed some police tape which appeared to be marking off a crime scene. Some flowers had also been laid on the ground. I asked what had happened there. We were informed that several KPS (Kosovo Police Service) officers who had been from our assigned station had been ambushed, and one was killed and one seriously wounded. This had occurred just days before our arrival. One of the officers in the car miraculously escaped the trap with his life.

Now, these are the details of the situation as it was later told to me by the two Canadian officers Marc Birs and Gordon McConnell. On November 24, 2003, at around 0800 hours, KPS officers Sabahate Tolaj, Isuf Haklaj, and Hysen Lataj were traveling from Decani towards Peja. They were ambushed by four subjects in a white Mercedes Benz and a white Audi; they wielded AK 47's. Tolaj, who was driving and was female, was killed; Haklaj, who was the front passenger, was seriously wounded in the neck and head. He was taken to the hospital in Pristina where he later died. Lataj was in the rear seat, and as said before, he escaped with his life. All available IPO(International Police Officer) , KPS, and KFOR(Kosovo Forces, name for multi-national military assigned there) resources were called in to search the area for the suspects, including K-9 and air support. One of the vehicles was found shortly after the incident, and several subjects were arrested in connection with the crime.

Sabahate Tolaj was apparently a very dedicated and hardworking investigator who tried to solve cases regardless of the victim or suspect's political beliefs or connections. She was investigating some very sensitive murder cases. One involved a former K.LA. Colonel, Tahir Zemaj, who was her commander during the war. Zemaj was murdered in Peja in January 2003. She was also investigating the murder of an Ilir Selimaj, who was a witness in the Zemaj case and a KPS Officer, Hajdar Ahmeti, who was murdered in Gjakova in August 2003. Tolaj was also involved in the case of Daut Haradinaj, a former K.LA. Officer convicted for his involvement in the murders of Kosovo Albanians during the war. Daut Haradinaj received fourteen years imprisonment and is the brother of Ramush Haradinaj (who we will discuss later in a little more detail.)

On November 25, a Decani KPS Officer, Sami Cacaj, was arrested for possible involvement in the murder of Tolaj and Haklaj. Apparently, Tolaj and Cacaj had had several arguments at the station in the past. Perhaps their biggest difference was the fact Tolaj was associated with the L.D.K. (Democratic League of Kosovo) political party and Cacaj was associated with the A.A.K (Alliance for the Future of Kosovo) party. There was a third party, the P.D.K. (Democratic Party of Kosovo). Now, I don't know the ends and outs of the three, only that each party has its own vision of Kosovo and how that end should be achieved. From what I was told, Sami Cacaj was handcuffed to a chair for twenty-four hours while he was questioned. He was released and never returned to Decani station.

Myself, Mark Lewis and Jason Hinds would work together and eventually become good friends. When we arrived in Decani, we met the station command staff. The station was a two-story gray building with two flags flying in front, one the blue and white U.N. flag and the other a

K.P.S. flag. Americans held two of the top positions, station commander and operations officer. The logistics officer was from India, the admin chief was from Jordan, the chief investigator was from Africa, and the intelligence officer, Henning Kremmin, was from Germany. We eventually became good friends through a mutual love of WWII history. His nickname was "the Pope." Now, I'm not going to pull any punches, before I went on this mission I was under the impression western cops were the best—best trained, best techniques, and best technology. After this mission, my fears were confirmed.

Now, I don't mean to disrespect any other country, but most countries are light-years behind the U.S., U.K., and Germany, when it comes to modern policing. I realize it was a U.N. mission and not a U.S. mission. The U.N. was so bent on a balance of nationality, they would not allow too many westerners to be in positions of authority. In my opinion, officers would be appointed to positions regardless of ability or, I should say, a lack thereof to maintain this balance. In all fairness, I'm not going to say that American officers have the monopoly on police work, and I'm by no means the sharpest tool in the shed.

Now the Kosovo mission was one to reestablish human rights, the rule of law, democratic policing, etc. Another thing that really confused me about the U.N. was how they allowed, say, countries from Africa, which had terrible human rights records, to send officers on these types of missions. But on the other side of that coin, there was also a lot of politics in the American contingent. This was my first mission, and I was naive for a brief time. I learned quickly that the good ole boy system was in effect. If you were prior mission and knew someone, you could get a much better assignment. Now, I had only learned about this kind of overseas work fairly recently. There were American officers that had already been on several missions. The Kosovo mission kicked off shortly after the war ended in 1999. There was also a mission in East Timor that had been going on for several years.

HOME SWEET HOME AWAY FROM HOME

After meeting the staff, the next issue was to find housing. This was actually a lot easier than I anticipated. This was accomplished with the help of a language assistant. Most of them were young men that were college educated or in college before the war. Their job was obviously to translate for us with the KPS officers and the local populace. Some would remain in the station to interpret, to translate reports and documents; the others would go out on patrol to interpret for us. There was one in particular that seemed capable to get about anything for you. I always wondered how much he was making on the side. If you needed a housekeeper, his aunt just so happened to be handy with a mop, broom, iron, or whatever you needed, and could keep your place tidy for a moderate sum, of course. If you needed heating fuel, he had a cousin who just happened to make propane deliveries. We looked at a few real rat holes before we found a suitable accommodation.

Mark and I ended up sharing a very nice two bedroom apartment. It was pretty new construction and modern as far as Kosovo was concerned. It had two bathrooms, a kitchen, and a living room area. The floor had a greenish colored carpet, and the windows were covered with orange velour curtains. All it needed was a strobe light and disco ball. There were no real cupboards to speak of and no pantry in the kitchen. There was about enough room to store food for a couple of days. The refrigerator was big enough to put a few drinks and some eggs in, not much more. It didn't exactly keeps things ice cold either, cool but definitely not cold. We usually put things out on the balcony to keep cold in the snow. The stove was a small electric affair. It took about a half an hour to boil a pot of water and several hours to bake anything.

The bedrooms were decent, and all the furniture was brand new. I had a large bed with a down-type mattress, a large armoire, and bedside tables. It was quite comfy and cozy. The bathrooms were also pretty nice with tile floors. The toilet and fixtures were nice white porcelain with a shell design. Now, I don't know who designed the shower, but it had several flaws. It was against the outer wall which angled inward to the ceiling; when I showered, I had to hunch over. There was also a window there, so unless you wanted the neighbors to see you in your birthday suit, you had to cover it, which I did with aluminum foil. It also had a pedestal-type basin, and more water went on the floor than down the drain. Each bathroom had a small hot water heater mounted on the wall. They held about enough hot water for a shower and not much more.

There was also a small washing machine. It was big enough to wash a uniform, a pair of socks, underwear, and a t-shirt. You really couldn't get much more than that in to it at one time. The building had a steam radiator-type heating system; unfortunately, the landlord was too cheap to fire up the boiler. He did provide two electric heaters. Two problems with that: they didn't put out enough heat to warm a room, and there were frequent power outages in Kosovo. Mark and I went out and bought a couple of propane heaters in order to keep from freezing to death. They did a good job, but getting the tanks refilled was a hassle. The living room had a brown velour sectional with a TV hooked up to a satellite dish that never worked. Overall, it was a comfortable place to live. The apartment cost us each 225 Euro a month. At the time, I think it was about 200 bucks a month apiece. I don't remember the conversion rate, but that couldn't have been too shabby for the landlord. We looked at some apartments which were pretty cheap to rent but unfortunately they were real rat holes. We found out that most landlords would charge officers from western countries more than officers from say Africa or India. They assumed we had more money. They especially charged Americans more because they knew our standard of living was higher, and everyone knows all Americans are rich.

DECANI: QUAINT LAND OF ENCHANTMENT

Decani was a quaint little farming community. There was one paved road which was the main drag running through the town. On the main drag were some grocery stores, a barber shop, a couple of little coffee houses, a pizzeria, a few other various shops, and the police station. It was a fairly clean town, all things considered. There were some side streets that were pretty trashy, though. There was also a high school, a hospital, and the city hall. The mountains to the west of town were very gorgeous, especially once winter dropped a beautiful thick blanket of white all over them and the town. Now, I'm a Florida boy, and I thought it was cold in Germany and the snow thick when I was in the army. But it was seriously cold, and it snowed by the foot there. The Serbian monastery also gave it a medieval air. There was a road running off the main drag called Market Road; it was of interest because every Thursday all the locals came here to sell their wares. There were fresh fruits, vegetables, honey, live poultry, livestock, and every other kind of goods you could want.

I was assigned to a patrol squad of four other International Police Officers. The team leader was a big friendly guy from Fiji, an officer from Jordan who smoked like a chimney, an officer from India, and one from Africa. All were decent people. Now, I must admit the team leader, although he didn't look very impressive in uniform, really knew the area. I started out on night shift. We went on patrol, and this guy knew the A.O. (Area of Operation) like the back of his hand. Most of the roads were dirt, and there were so many twists and turns and side roads and cow paths, I had no idea where I was when the shift ended. He even showed me a hotel that was several stories tall in the forest. Apparently it was started in the 1970s as a resort but was never finished. Reportedly, there's good skiing up in the mountains in that area. During one shift I was asking him what type of weapon he was carrying. Turns out he had an old pre-WWII Smith and Wesson .38 caliber revolver. He told me before he was deployed, they took these guns out of a Fijian museum for their officers to use. Apparently officers in Fiji didn't carry firearms. He took it out and opened the cylinder which was empty. I asked him about the officer safety issue of carrying an unloaded weapon. He said the gun was safer that way. I left it at that.

TRAGEDY STRIKES BACK HOME

I was only there a few days and really getting settled in when I found out my mom had died. My wife sent me an email telling me to call right away. When I called, she asked me if I had gotten her message. I asked her, "What message?" She broke the bad news to me and told me mom had died on the sixth. She told me she had talked to the Red Cross and the "company," trying to get a hold of me. I was impressed at how fast my station commander got the ball rolling to get me home. I actually left that day and went home for about ten days for my mom's funeral. It was pretty painful obviously. Mom had been ill for several years and had worsened before I left. The doctors had given her a year or so to live. Obviously no one can put a date on death except God Almighty. Even though you know it's coming, it's never easy to lose a loved one even when you know they're suffering and going to a better place. I felt a good amount of guilt for not being there when my mom passed even though she had given me her blessing. Mom had had a hard life. Her dad had abandoned them, her mom died after her birth, she was adopted, and from what she told me, they weren't a very loving family and were extremely harsh and strict. My dad was an alcoholic, and Mom struggled for years, trying to help him until his death at a fairly early age of forty-five. My grandmother wasn't exactly supportive of my mom, either. Mom wasn't always as understanding or outwardly loving sometimes, but she did her best under the circumstances. She maintained her faith in God and took every opportunity to pass it on to me. Her funeral was very nice, and I was deeply touched by the fact that many of my former co-workers and friends from the Clay County Sheriff's Office came to her funeral.

I RETURN TO KOSOVO

Returning to Kosovo was a difficult decision. Under the circumstances, I wasn't really in the mindset to leave my family and deal with my grief in a strange country and with people I really didn't know. However, I got my thoughts together and decided not to quit, and I returned around the eighteenth. My roommate, Mark Lewis, was very supportive and understanding. We did celebrate Christmas with a little decorated artificial tree and some presents sent from home. Much of the remainder of the month was spent getting settled in my living quarters and trying to learn the area. As I said before, it was a pretty serious winter. It snowed several feet, and the area was covered. The road department did a good job of keeping the main road drivable. Most of the officers from Africa and India generally did not really like to drive and even less so in the snow. Most loved having an American on their team because they knew we loved to drive. The "Coca-Colas" were red and white Toyota Forerunners. They were six-cylinder, four-wheel drive vehicles. They had a blue rotating light on top. What most old time cops would call a bubble gum machine. They were excellent vehicles. Probably the best decision the U.N. ever made.

THE ITALIANS

The Italian KFOR (Kosovo Forces) had control of this area. Their main camp was about halfway between Decani and

Peja. They had a smaller camp and detachment locally to protect the monastery. Remember, Decani is made up of Albanian Muslims, and the monastery is Orthodox Christian with Serbian monks. You get the picture. The local Italian detachment was housed in what was some type of youth camp. The current command staff at the station apparently hadn't cultivated much rapport with the Italians. The station commander and the ops chief were old timers, and I eventually learned they both had a pretty bad alcohol problem. The station commander always had a cup in his hand. His cup was always full of vodka and some type of juice. The ops guy didn't drink continually, but when he did, he got hammered and apparently had a bad temper.

Once these guys were gone, we were able to develop a great working relationship with the Italian officers. Two officers in particular were Lt. Rocco "The Rock" Larocca and a Captain Alessandro "White Horse" Bianco. They were very eager to work with us and were extremely amicable. They were quite the characters, too. It got to the level of them inviting us to their chow hall, letting us shoot their weapons on the range, and they even let us drive one of their tanks. I spent a couple of years in the armored cavalry, so this was a treat for me. I could never talk them into letting me fire the main gun, though.

I also had the pleasure of meeting one of their intelligence officers, who we shared information with on more than one occasion. He was Italian obviously but had one Korean parent and looked more Asian than anything. He was quite a character and spoke several languages. To this day, I don't know his name; we called him "the Turtle." Anytime we were at some ceremony or whatever, this guy would appear out of nowhere. It was kind of scary sometimes. My mission initially consisted of working with and training the KPS and doing joint house searches/raids and checkpoints with the Italians. At that time, U.N. Resolution 1244 was in place. Basically that gave a lot of freedom to conduct searches for illegal weapons, etc with little or no probable cause. It was every American defense attorney's nightmare. I loved it.

In fact, I was involved in one such joint operation late in December. The bad guys were fairly clever at hiding stuff. We found weapons in dog houses, wells, wood piles, buried in the garden, etc. We conducted or assisted in searches on a regular basis. Another situation we faced fairly often were UXO'S (Unexploded Ordinance). We responded on numerous occasions to a farmer or other local who had found a live RPG (Rocket Propelled Grenade), mortar round, land mine, or hand grenade in their field et cetera. This increased in the spring when the farmers began to plow their fields for the planting season.

GETTING INTO THE GROOVE AND MAKING FRIENDS

My routine at first was basically patrolling around the area and trying to enjoy my time off. Now, it was cold, and power outages were fairly frequent. So you invested in some type of wood burning stove or propane heaters, which Mark and I had done. There wasn't much outside activity to get involved in. I also tried to get to know the KPS Officers and language assistants. Many of them told stories about their hardships at the hands of the Yugoslavian military or police. Family members arrested, murdered, tortured, etc. Also many of them told stories about, at the height of the conflict, having to flee to the mountains in the winter with little or no food, clothing, etc. Some pretty rough stories.

Also, as I said before, I became friends with "the Pope" and several of the other German officers at the station. I had been stationed in Germany in the 80s in the army. So I loved the food, the beer, and Germany in general. I had learned just enough of the language to order a beer, some food, find the train station, and get my face slapped. So "the Pope" and the other Germans helped me when I expressed an interest in learning more of their language. Now, I know you're asking, why in the world you would want to learn German in Kosovo? Well, it turns out that it was beneficial. Many people fled from Kosovo to Germany before and during the war. So at times I was able to communicate more on my own without the help of a translator. When the spring came, we turned the German lessons into quite an enjoyable endeavor. Two of the Germans lived at an apartment that had a very nice garden for enjoying some good food and drink. Another enjoyable get-together was a big pancake breakfast we shared. Marc and Gordon had acquired some good Canadian maple syrup, so we got together one Sunday morning and cooked a huge stack of pancakes and enough bacon to put an elephant into cardiac arrest. When you're thousands of miles from home and family, any excuse to get together with guys you have things in common with can't be passed up. There was one Indian officer named Sanjeev who was a very nice guy and an excellent cook. He invited several of us to his accommodations on a few occasions for dinner. He made some awesome curry chicken.

DECANI AND THE WAR FOR FREEDOM

As I said before, the Peja region and Decani in particular played a very big part in the fight against Milosevic. I actually had the "pleasure" of meeting one of the leaders of this movement. His name was Ramush Haradinaj. He was a leader of the K.L.A. or Kosovo Liberation Army. He was born in Gllogjan (glow-john) a village in the area of Decani. He had served in the Yugoslavian military and was well educated. He was instrumental in organizing forces, smuggling weapons from Albania, and procuring funds to support it all. He was also a ground force commander. He lived in the area still and was considered a very big hero to the people. I actually read a book about him called *A Narrative about War and Freedom* while I was there. It's important to learn how people think and feel, especially about their icons. During the war, it's apparent, I think, both sides committed their fair share of atrocities. I saw at least one U.N. intelligence memo with photos from a Serb newspaper, showing K.L.A. soldiers holding the severed heads of Serbian soldiers. From what I heard, Haradinaj was involved in a few himself. I was told there's a lake in the area full of Serbs and Albanians alike that had crossed him. After the war, he was involved in the political process, primarily the A.A.K. political party, and became Prime Minister of Kosovo. He has been arrested in recent years, and it will be up to the courts to decide his guilt or innocence, I suppose.

CULTURE CLASH

As I said before, ethnic Albanians are generally of the Islamic faith. There were numerous mosques in the area. Now, in my experience, it seemed this was true more so for the older citizens. Many of our language assistants, who were mostly younger men, talked of going to Pristina and partying, which included lots of drinking and prostitutes. Again, Decani was predominantly a farming community and much more conservative and traditional than a large city like Pristina. The young women in many ways were guarded as you would expect in most Muslim countries. There were a few female KPS officers and language assistants. They were, however, treated with a degree of reservation and skepticism. Sabahate Tolaj, who was mentioned earlier, may have been an exception to the rule. They were not supposed to be in the company of a male who was not a relative without a chaperone, not allowed any physical contact, etc. Now, when I learned this, I was very surprised because many of the young women were very attractive and dressed in a very modern fashion. Many of them looked like they belonged in a European fashion magazine—tight sweaters, jeans, etc. Now, many of the families were very traditional and close-knit. Blood feuds and honor killings were still very much in their mindset. In fact, many times serious crimes such as shootings were settled among feuding families. This was usually accomplished by some kind of payoff or other agreement. There were also situations when a young male would be beaten up for a violation of some young lady's honor. I saw the cultural contradictions; some trying to maintain the old ways while the younger trying to move towards a more modern, more Western lifestyle.

JANUARY

During the month of January, it continued to be cold with more snow. The roofs of the houses were covered in a thick blanket of white. The power lines, sagging from the weight of the ice, would snap and give a little light show. The balcony on the west side of my apartment gave an excellent view of the mountains. There were days when the snowfall was so thick and heavy, you literally couldn't see them. Some days the clouds covered the face of the mountain like a lace wedding veil. The station conducted numerous house or business searches and checkpoints with the Italian KFOR during the month. On the twenty-fourth, a ceremony was held at a local cemetery to inter the body of local man named Sinan Musaj. This man had been a member of one of the local crime families that had been murdered by a rival family. Now, the rumor I heard was this guy was snuffed by someone in the Ramush Haridinaj family. I don't know if that was true or if any arrests were ever made.

On the surface, Decani was a quiet, somewhat of a picturesque place. However, there was quite a bit of underlying criminal activity all over Kosovo. A lot of this activity was a continuation of involvement in the K.L.A. or other crime activity which arose during the war such as black marketeers. There was a degree of illegal drugs, black market fuel, prostitution, and illegal weapons. A lot of the illegal weapons were caches from the war along with new arms being moved. Kosovo wanted its independence from Serbia, and most people in Kosovo were holding on to their weapons to that end. I guess they figured if they couldn't get it peacefully, they'd take it. Or they figured at some point in time, the Serbs from that area that had been displaced would return. They would need those weapons for payback, I guess.

On January 27, I was transferred from a patrol team and

made chief of the (ten man) traffic unit. Now, as a deputy, I performed basic traffic enforcement duties but was by no means an expert. I was never a traffic homicide investigator or traffic crash reconstructionist. It was more title than expertise, I assure you. These guys were by far the best and most motivated of all the officers of the station. I basically went on patrol with these guys and showed them how to do traffic stops, vehicle searches, and checkpoints. They did well overall. The main problem I encountered was their ideas about officer safety. They were terrible about turning their backs on what I or most American officers would consider a suspect. They wouldn't keep a reactionary gap or what most would call their personal space. They would actually hug drivers they'd stopped. I'd ask them, "What are you doing?" *Oh, it's okay. He's a friend of my third cousin's uncle twice removed. He's okay. No problem.* It was almost impossible to drill that through their heads. But it's difficult to undue culture.

FEBRUARY

It was decided that since the traffic unit was a little more motivated and had a little more on the ball than most of their fellow officers that they would be used to serve arrest warrants. So I arranged with the training unit to put on some basic SWAT type training on building entry and room clearance and searches. The IPO (International Police Officer) assigned to the training unit was one of the Canadian officers. He had a pretty extensive background as a narcotics officer and had conducted numerous high risk raids and searches. We did some classroom instruction then spent several hours doing practical exercises. We had no real training facilities locally, so we had to improvise. Improvisation was a necessity on this mission. There was an old abandoned industrial pump factory just north of town which served the purpose. I was told that it was hit by a U.S. warplane, and supposedly after the war, the pilot actually came to Decani to see his handy work.

One pleasure I did look forward to was a periodic trip to Camp Bondsteel. Bondsteel was the American Kosovo Forces base, complete with PX and a Burger King. It was located south of Pristina and several hours away. I visited there for the second time in February. There were several grocery stores in Decani which provided fresh fruits and vegetables, canned goods, etc. There was also a butcher shop, but I was a little leery of that. I have to admit, I ate more than my fair share of noodles, jarred tomato sauce, and pizza. But the few times I and any of the other Americans at the station could sneak away for a shopping trip was a real treat. Nacho dip and Fritos were at a premium. Of course the trip isn't complete without a double whopper with cheese. Now, the ultimate highlight of February was the leave I took in Frankfurt with my wife for a week. A week of good food, sightseeing, and a big warm bed in the fatherland was a welcome reprieve. The warm bed part was especially appreciated because when I returned, Mark was telling about how cold it was when I was away. He told me there was no power in Decani for several days because of the weather. He said he and several other IPO's went to a hotel in Peja so they could get a hot bath and some relief from the cold.

MARCH

Now, as I mentioned before, Kosovo is filled with monuments to this or that battle or this or that fallen hero; they are numerous. Decani is no exception. Monuments are everywhere. In fact in Gllogjan, home of K.L.A. great Ramush Haradinaj, there is a large monument and cemetery. It seemed there was a ceremony weekly to honor some fallen hero. On March 4, there was one such ceremony. On the twenty-fourth, there was a large ceremony at the Gllogjan monument to commemorate the sixth anniversary of the start of the war. The monument itself is a large, beautiful four-story stone and mortar structure. Inside the walls are covered with what looked to me like cedar. The structure is supposed to be a replica of houses built in the region centuries ago. The ceremony was quite a large affair with several thousands in attendance and traditional dancers. This is when I met Ramush Haradinaj. Should have asked for an autograph, but I didn't think of it at the time. On the other side of the coin, there were numerous protests in regard to some former K.L.A. member who had been arrested for some atrocity or for one who was already imprisoned. March 16 marked one such protest.

My mission so far had been relatively quiet and uneventful. Most of my time, I spent with the station's traffic unit, doing checkpoints, patrols, and chasing illegal woodcutters. Now, you may laugh at this, but actually, illegal woodcutting was a very lucrative enterprise. Most of the woodcutters took it very seriously, too. Like I said previously, there was no real industry, so the locals were generally looking for some type of endeavor to sustain them in addition to farming. Trees could be harvested legally, but the person had to have papers from the K.F.A. (Kosovo Forestry Authority), and there was a limit. The trees had to be marked by the K.F.A. before they were cut then stamped on the ends after they were cut. Now, I'm sure there was some corruption involved here, and the stamps were not hard to duplicate. There were also numerous saw mills in the area, and they had to be licensed and inspected by the K.F.A.

RIOTS

I said my tour was so far uneventful—that is, until the riots in March from the seventeenth through the nineteenth. The riots started over some children that drowned in Mitrovica. Mitrovica is a town in northern Kosovo. I was never there, but my understanding was the town was part Albanian and part Serb, and the two parts were divided by the river that flowed through the city. Supposedly some Albanian kids were chased by two Serbian males and a dog, jumped in the river to get away, and three drowned. The riots went on for about three days. I did not witness this incident but was told about it firsthand. One American officer had to shoot and kill a rioter up in Peja. Apparently some of the rioters were trying to torch houses in a Serbian enclave. During this, an American officer was threatened with a concrete block or chunk of concrete, resulting in the shooting and death of the rioter. The officer was a female who I knew; she was in my group that came over from the States. I mentioned earlier blood feuds; well, you can imagine how irate this guy's family was that he had been killed and by a female on top of it. Well, apparently the officer received some death threats and had to be moved to another region. The final results of the riots were hundreds wounded, thirty or more killed, and untold homes and Serb churches were burned or destroyed.

On March 17th, several hundred rioters came to the police

station gate wanting to storm the building. I was on duty along with several other western officers and a handful of KPS. I think the officers from some of the other countries were inside, hiding under desks. Not sure, I was busy dodging rocks and bottles outside. There were also shots fired from somewhere in the crowd. It was a very tense situation. I had been in some pretty hairy situations as a cop but had never faced those kinds of numbers. The acting station commander, Mark Lewis, did a great job. He was able to placate the rioters by allowing them to take down the U.N. flag. It was that or they threatened to storm the station and burn it down. Once they got the flag, they burned it with great enthusiasm while others danced in the street. Hey, no biggie to me. It wasn't the American flag. That would have been much different to the few American officers present. The important thing is no one was hurt. There was no way we were going to be able to hold off that crowd without there being some people hurt or killed. The Italian military was unable to assist us until after the riots were over. They had been ordered to other areas of trouble. Although, later that night, an Italian convoy was fired at when it passed in front of my apartment building.

I said before that I felt the U.N. was an exercise in futility. Well, a couple of examples are as follows. Mark Lewis, the acting station commander, was later relieved. Not because he defused the situation by allowing the rioters to take down the U.N. flag, but because on March 18 and 19, protestors entered the station compound and put up an American flag, again under a threat of bloodshed. After an investigation, it was stated he didn't order the flag down quickly enough. During the riot, several officers from other countries acted in a blatantly cowardly manner. However, no action was taken against them, and to the best of my knowledge, no inquiry was made. The demonstrations on the eighteenth and nineteenth were pretty restrained compared to the seventeenth. On the nineteenth, the demonstrators were actually carrying an American flag along with the Albanian. As I said before, on this date an Albanian and American flag were raised by protestors at the police station again under threat of violence.

One officer, due to his poor judgment, was the cause for one of our "Coca-Colas" getting torched by rioters. Orders were given to keep all the vehicles in the compound, which he disobeyed. Again, nothing happened to this officer. I won't reveal what country these officers were from other than outside the United States. Several U.N. vehicles assigned to the city hall were also burned.

It's funny that the U.S. provided some of the best officers who did the majority of the work, and it seemed that if an officer from outside the western nations made a mistake they were more readily forgiven. If an American or officer from another western country made a mistake, it seemed the powers that be were more apt to punish them.

Well, I guess I've railed against the U.N. enough. On the night of the eighteenth, I believe, several mortar rounds were launched at the monastery but did no damage. We were fortunate no one was seriously hurt in our area. Other than the burned vehicles and the incident at the station, most of the activity in Decani was limited to organized protestors marching up and down the main street. Mostly chanting in Albanian, of course, "Down with the U.N. and OU CHA KA" (UCK, Albanian for K.L.A.) and "Mitrovica!"

A lot of the organizers were former K.L.A. There was one former K.L.A., Avdyl Mushkolaj, who was a real pain in the butt. During any ceremony or protest and during the riots, he was in the thick of things. He was eventually arrested on April 12 in Decani. The U.N. actually had a fair special operations unit that snatched him up. This event almost caused a riot in itself. I and several other officers were required by the district prosecutor in Peja to give statements to all I had observed in regards to Mushkolaj's activities. One of the prosecutors assigned to the case was an American.

In general, most of the locals were glad that NATO had bombed the Serbs and ended the war; there was a faction that resented the U.N.'s presence, though. The former K.L.A. members still exercised a lot of influence. In fact, many of the locals had been members, including the KPS. This is why most of the IPO's took everything the KPS said or did with a grain of salt. I always felt they had ulterior motives, especially if they seemed too cooperative. The KPS commander, Captain Ahmet Hasi, was nice enough, but he seemed too fearful to exert much influence or control. Now, the KPS operations officer, Ramadan Boshtraj, was pretty forceful. At times, he seemed to carry more weight than the actual commander.

Ramadan was very respectful, especially to Americans. I and several other officers ate dinner at his home with his family on several occasions. He was always a very gracious host and would give you anything in his home. Remember the mural of Clinton in Pristina? Well, Ramadan had a picture of the former president himself prominently displayed on his wall. As a guest, I learned not to eat or drink too fast because they would always fill your plate or cup with more. Now, from what I saw, the men loved their cigarettes (most smoked like chimneys), their coffee, and their rockia. Now, rockia was very strong liquor you drank in shots, and I believe it was made out of plums. To me, it tasted like aviation fuel. The first time I choked a shot down, everyone laughed and said, "Good, no? You must drink more!" Needless to say, after a couple shots, I was feeling quite warm inside.

They also like their coffee—Turkish coffee in particular. Turkish coffee comes in a small glass resembling a shot glass. It's made with coffee, obviously, that's finely ground like flour. The water and coffee are put into a small copper pot and boiled. You end up with about an inch of liquid and two inches of sludge in the bottom or your glass. Well, the first time I drank some, I didn't realize you had to let it sit for a minute or so for the grounds to settle to the bottom. So I ended up with a mouthful of grounds. After a while, I can't say I really liked it, but I tolerated it. The old saying goes, when in Rome, do as the Romans do, at least enough so as not to insult your host. The last I heard Ramadan and his family were living in New York.

Mark Lewis had been the acting station commander during the riots and had been relieved of his position as deputy commander. He was replaced by a guy from Peja named Tim Winterhalter. He was American. He was also big, loud, boisterous, and funny as all get out. You couldn't help but like the guy. He was brutally honest with IPOs and KPS alike. He was a former army ranger and SWAT guy from Tampa, Florida. You wouldn't think it to look at him. But like Cartman says, "I'm not fat; I'm big boned!" Tim moved pretty well on the basketball court, too. The last time I spoke to him, he was in Afghanistan.

ATTACK AT MITROVICA

There were some other incidents in the month of March that were significant. On the eighteenth, a tragedy unfolded which caused a great deal of shock and suspicion amongst the IPOs. We did not get news of this until after the riots were over. A group of IPOs assigned at the Mitrovica Detention Center were leaving the prison after a day of training. Apparently when the bus carrying the officers out was stopped in between the sally port gates, a Jordanian S.P.U. (Special Police Unit) guard opened up on the bus with an AK-47. The Jordanian S.P.U. was responsible for security of the facility. Rumors spread like wildfire. The story we received through the grapevine was that the Jordanian opened fire for obviously no apparent provocation, and one of the other S.P.U. guards was handing him magazines through the fence when he needed to reload. While this was unfolding, the other S.P.U. guards were standing by, doing nothing to stop it. Now, I'm not clear on who returned fire, but the gunman was killed. Two American officers were killed, ten were wounded, and one Austrian officer was seriously wounded. Four Jordanian S.P.U.s were detained for possible involvement or for the lack of action in the incident.

There was a memorial service in Pristina a couple of days after the shooting. I and several other officers from Decani were able to attend. I remember a lot of big speeches being made by some of the top U.N. police contingent officers about getting to the bottom of the incident and punishing those responsible. Well, shortly thereafter the four Jordanians were released and cleared of any "misconduct." Are you kidding me? Misconduct a U.N. euphemism for murder? I have to believe it was more U.N. incompetence or not wanting to upset our Middle Eastern friends. It's all about national balance. Maybe they figured we had too many officers in country. Let me clarify something. I did not know any of the officers killed or wounded and consider them all brother or sister police officers. My beef is with the U.N. and its dismal achievements. That's only my opinion. I'm sure there are plenty out there who think the U.N. is the next best thing to sliced bread.

At least one got his just desserts. Although, I never heard what the motive was—maybe some perceived insult by one of the Americans or some other westerner. Who knows? Now, we had several Jordanians at the station. I do know of one who personally apologized to every American for the actions of his fellow countrymen. I told him thank you, but it wasn't his fault. He said he felt very bad and that he personally liked Americans and felt most of his fellow officers did too. There were several other Jordanian officers at the station who I think secretly reveled at the death of the American infidels although they never verbalized it.

IPO AMBUSHED

On the twenty-fourth, a U.N. police patrol was ambushed in the Pristina area, resulting in the deaths of a KPS Officer and one U.N. IPO from Ghana, and one language assistant was seriously wounded. Again, rumors spread like wildfire. Supposedly after the IPO and KPS officer were killed, the language assistant took one of the slain officer's guns and returned fire, apparently wounding one suspect. A body was found shortly after the incident and linked to the murder. A few days later, four suspects were arrested for possible involvement in the ambush. Generally, the bad guys didn't target the U.N. IPOs They kept pretty busy killing themselves and their rivals. Language assistants were obviously at risk in that some resented the U.N.'s presence and would consider them collaborators. They did a great job, but as I said previously, I always looked for ulterior motives. On the twenty-sixth, the station conducted a large operation consisting of checkpoints at some of the main road intersections in the area. March had been a very tumultuous month, not only for the U.N. CIVPOL, but for all the people of Kosovo. It raised many questions as to the security status and if peace between the Serbs and ethnic Albanians would ever be possible.

APRIL

Now, as spring came, the temperature rose; the snow melted which made things a muddy mess in areas. Although the snow melted, you could still see snow caps on the mountains. The trees were turning green again, the flowers were budding and blooming, and the bees were buzzing—you get the picture. Now that the weather was turning nice, it gave an opportunity to get outside and enjoy the scenery. As far as operations, it wasn't an extremely busy month. We conducted one on the first consisting of checkpoints at road junctions, typical vehicle searches for illegal weapons, etc. We also received intelligence of a possibility that protests might take place on the twenty-ninth due to a subject in Mitrovica being arrested. Nothing of serious incident occurred in our area. I did my normal patrols with the traffic unit and chased woodcutters on a fairly regular basis.

So April was a pretty quiet month for me in general—that is, compared to the preceding month. When you have time on your hands, you do what you can to occupy it constructively: read, watch DVDs, write letters, or hope you get a nice care package from home. The company I worked for had a "clubhouse," for a lack of a better word, in every region staffed by a full-time logistics person. Ours was in Peja. We would usually make a trip once a week if possible. The logistics guy was there to give us our mail, take our outgoing mail, and our time sheets once a month. There was also a library of books and DVDs we could check out. Dennis was our logistics man; he was a great guy. He had an apartment that was part of the "clubhouse." He lived there with his wife who was Filipino, and I think he said they had a pineapple plantation. She was very nice; they frequently threw barbeques for all the Americans in the region. Now, he had it good. He had his wife with him, and the company paid for their apartment. It just doesn't get much better than that.

Some of the other officers and I were able to take a trip to Rugova Pass west of Peja. It's a beautiful mountain gorge with a river running through it. There are meadows and sheer rock cliffs and snow-capped peaks. The road winds around the mountain, crossing the gorge over old stone bridges and snakes through tunnels cut from the rock. Towards the top is a small resort called "Rugova Camp." There was a nice little restaurant and several cabins or chalets you could rent. There was a tank fed by a stream full of fish from which you could choose your dinner. One incident did occur that I guess I will attribute to comic relief. On the seventeenth, we received three new American officers at the station. I was tasked with driving them around the area to get them familiarized. We were traveling on the monastery road when I noticed some freshly cut logs across a stream. Well, the stream didn't appear too deep, so I decided to cross. Well, it was deeper, and the streambed was soft, so I ended up stuck. We locked the four-wheel drive hubs, and I rocked the vehicle back and forth for several minutes to no avail. I called Jason Hinds on my cell phone for assistance. After about a half an hour, he arrived. By this time I had told the new officers to get out and stand on the bank. The water was rising in the vehicle, and I figured since I was the "captain," it was up to me to go down with my ship. Jason arrived to help and I hooked a tow rope to the vehicle so he could pull me out. Unfortunately the bank was covered in loose gravel and Jason's "coca-cola" couldn't get enough traction. He went to the Italian camp and came back with some soldiers who pulled me out. By this time, though, the water was about over the seats, and I was soaked from the waist down and freezing. The vehicle kept running the whole time. Those were some good trucks. The only real casualty was the radio which got fried out in the water. The upholstery was soaked, of course. Fortunately, we were allowed to trade it for a newer one shortly thereafter. Now, I was pretty embarrassed by all this. I figured these guys thought I was a real knucklehead. What a way to start them off. They took it in stride and with good humor. In fact, there's always a real joker in the group. One of them swore when it came time to write a statement for the incident report, he would attest that IPO Little's (that's me) last words before entering the stream were "hold my beer and watch this." I figured I'd be in Kosovo for the next five years paying for the "Coca-Cola."

MAY

Now, the illegal woodcutters were pretty dedicated to their craft. I tried to figure out a way to make some progress with this problem. I wanted to do some night operations and was able to get a pair of night vision goggles, AN/PVS-5, for you former military guys. I signed them out from the regional logistics officer. On the seventh, I was reassigned from the traffic unit to supervise a KPS investigations task force to try to address the woodcutting issue. Now, this meant I had a few KPS officers at my disposal and was allowed to patrol the forests in the mountains on a daily basis where the wood was being cut. I took leave from the eleventh through the twenty-fourth. My son was graduating from high school, and I could not miss that. It's always a time of pride and tears to see your kids pass a milestone in their life. Now, this was the first time I was home since my mom's funeral, so of course you try to cram as much stuff into the shortest time possible. So when my leave was up, as always, it was difficult to leave.

When I returned, I was still assigned to the task force and continued my efforts to catch the illegal woodcutters and continued to patrol. We made several arrests and confiscated hundreds of cubic feet of cut logs. Now, I had briefly mentioned before our original station commander and operations chief. They left around the end of February for the States. Our new commander was an Indian officer. He had thick black hair and sideburns. His nick name was—yes, you guessed it—Elvis. Now, Mark Lewis was acting station commander during the riots because "Elvis" was on leave and Mark was relieved as deputy commander. Jason Hinds was promoted to Operations Chief and eventually became Deputy Station Commander. On the twenty-eighth, the opening for the operations job was posted. I applied and of course didn't get it. At the end of the month, regional headquarters requested some grid coordinates for some of the woodcutting areas. So I took my GPS into the woods and plotted some areas being hit pretty hard. I was informed that I would be allowed to schedule a U.N. flight over the area to photograph the spots being ravaged by the woodcutters.

JUNE

On June 5, some of the other officers at the station and I received a letter from the Italian KFOR, thanking us for our cooperation, hard work, etc. It's always nice to get a pat on the back. On the nineteenth and twentieth, there was a fairly big operation in Decani. The new Serb Orthodox Bishop was to be inaugurated at the Decani Monastery, and we were to assist the Italian KFOR with security. Now, this meant several busloads of Serbs would be coming through en route to the monastery. Now, overall there were no problems except some protesting and some rocks being thrown at one of the buses. All things considered, it could have been much worse. On the twenty-fifth, I took that U.N. flight over the area. I had to drive to Pristina to the U.N. airfield. The chopper was an old Russian made "MI-8 Hip," which was a troop trans-port. I had my doubts since the thing must have been thirty years old, and who knows how well it had been maintained? I'd have no problem getting into a U.S. military aircraft that old because I know we maintain our equipment. The thing was noisy and "rattley," but that's par for the course for a lot of helicopters, or at least the ones I've ever flown in. The flight was really great, I got a view of Kosovo I hadn't seen before and most other officers wouldn't get. The farms, lakes, rivers, towns, and villages looked like a postcard picture.

It was very informative and helpful to see Decani from the air, the town itself, the monastery, and the mountains around it. The mountains were even more awesome from above, and to fly between the peaks and through the clouds was really cool. Now, I had seen several areas from the ground that had been illegally cut, at least the ones we could reach. But to see it from the air really drove the magnitude of it home. You wouldn't think that some guys with axes, or maybe a chainsaw if they were lucky, could wreak so much havoc on the environment. It was bigger than I had realized or imagined. There were acres of land that had been stripped bare. Some of the areas were inaccessible to us, even in a four-wheel drive vehicle. I photographed the damaged areas, and these photos were submitted to regional HQ. Now, after this, a U.N. representative working with the K.F.A. came to Decani, asking to see the areas affected. He said he would do all he could to get more I.P.L.O.'s (International Police Liason Officer), vehicles, and money to try to stem the tide of the woodcutting. He told me that if it wasn't stopped, it could have serious environmental impact, erosion, and landslides. Well, I never saw it, and I would venture a guess they are still waiting for all this help from the U.N. On the twenty-sixth, we conducted an operation to attempt to arrest three subjects in a nearby village that had threatened some of the KPS officers at our station. If memory serves me correctly, all three were arrested without incident.

JULY

My daughter had a son, my first grandchild on the first of July. So I did the traditional passing out the cigars thing and had a couple celebratory drinks with some of the other officers. My son had graduated in May, and as a present, I had promised to meet him in Germany for about a week. His last two years of school, he had befriended an exchange student from Germany. The young man, Sebastian, and his family had invited us to visit them. They lived outside Hanover and had offered for us to stay with them. It was probably one of the nicest times I ever had in Germany. Sebastian's mom treated us like kings; every meal was a buffet, and you couldn't eat enough. Mom kept filling your plate up. After dinner, Dad broke out the drink, beer, schnapps, liquor, and wine. There was a drink called Dr. Bonekamp. It was like a liqueur in a little brown bottle. I can't describe the taste. Supposedly they were good for the digestion; well, I can tell you I had a healthy stomach that week. Sebastian's family also put on a good old-fashioned Fourth of July barbeque for us, complete with hamburgers, hotdogs, etc. We made a day trip to Bergen Belsen, one of the more notorious concentration camps; we also went to a museum near the former East German border. My son, Sebastian, and I took a trip by train to Berlin for a couple of days. We took a sightseeing tour and did some shopping. Some of the buildings are still damaged from WWII and have been left that way as a reminder. We also went to "Checkpoint Charlie," the crossing point from West to East Berlin in the American sector during the Cold War. For a buck, they'll stamp your passport. It was a good time, and it gave my son and me some time to do some "male bonding."

BACK FROM GERMANY

I returned on the tenth of July. When I returned, the "war" on illegal woodcutting raged on. They were still raping the forest, and we were still trying to stop them. We were winning—okay, we weren't winning, but we weren't losing either. We were doing the best we could with what we had. I had to hand it to them; they had the advantage in that they knew the area better than I ever would. They were clever, patient, and resourceful. They had trails and routes that you couldn't get through in a vehicle; you could barely get through on horse cart. They had lookouts, and I wouldn't be a bit surprised if someone at the station wasn't feeding them information. I generally tried to keep my plans as secret as possible, only telling one of the other American officers what I was doing. We had made numerous arrests and confiscated horses, carts, tractors, and probably thousands of cubic feet of lumber. The lumber was to be auctioned publicly, and some of the money was to go back into the KPS coffers. I had my doubts about the transparency of that system.

The K.F.A. was supposed to assist us in recovering logs and inform us when they saw any illegal activity. Well, as far as recovering logs, that seldom happened. There was always some excuse: no fuel for the chainsaws, no personnel, no truck. The station actually had a large logging truck that had been confiscated or found abandoned—I don't remember which. Some of us even put our own money into getting it fixed at least once. In all fairness to the K.F.A., resources and funds were limited, but I can't help but think corruption played a part and probably intimidation did too. Another issue was the fact that illegal logging was a minor offense, and most of the time, the perpetrators and their equipment were released quickly by the judge. Again, I have to wonder how much corruption or intimidation played into it. On occasion, we'd get lucky, and the judge would hold someone for a longer period if we had confiscated a large amount of lumber and equipment. We were trying to get the judges to treat it as an organized criminal enterprise rather than just individual acts; most of the guys we arrested more than once and many were associated with each other in these activities. Now, all of this would be much more exciting if I was talking about drug or weapons dealers, and I agree. Not what I had in mind when I came to the "wild west" of Kosovo. Hey, I guess everyone does his or her little part in the bigger picture.

DOG HUNTS

This next subject I put here for a lack of a better place to stick it. There was another war waged in the Decani area. There was a large population of wild dogs in the area and I'm sure all over Kosovo. They were everywhere: in the town, the outlying villages, in the mountain, etc. They were all over the place. They were a definite nuisance, dangerous on occasion, and a health issue. They ravaged through the trash, barked and howled constantly, roamed and fought in packs, and on occasion bit people, making possible rabies an issue. Well, there was a solution. All you P.E.T.A. fans or tree-hugging hippies hold on for this one. There was a local hunt club, and about once a month or so, there would be a dog hunt which was to the best of my knowledge sanctioned by the U.N. Now, I like animals as much as anyone but not to extremes. Under the circumstances, there weren't any other choices; there were other, more pressing issues to address before hiring dog catchers and setting up animal shelters. So when these hunts were conducted, usually a KPS and a U.N. police patrol would escort the hunters around the area. They'd ride around, blasting these poor dogs for several hours. Fortunately, I never had to participate in one. I remember lying in bed and hearing the shots ring out. There'd be a shot and sometimes silence. Many times it would be followed by bloodcurdling yelping and howling followed by another shot then silence. While this went on, there was supposed to be a truck or tractor with a trailer following the procession around to pick up the carcasses. Usually, though, for days there'd be dead dogs everywhere. It was a pretty nasty sight. I wonder why no one opened up any new restaurants.

GUARD SHACKS

On the fourteenth, I was reassigned to patrol because of a man power shortage. I still continued to patrol, looking for woodcutters, just not as much. It had been suggested long before I arrived in country to build some static guard shacks along the monastery road to try to stop or slow down the flow of wood being taken from the forests. There were several fording points along the stream adjacent to the road which led into Decani.

The shacks were finally started around June and completed in July. These were poorly built and had no electricity, water, toilet, or provision for trash collection. Before they were even manned, someone tried to burn one of them down. Once they were manned by KPS, the woodcutters started to cross the stream at other points out of view of the shacks. It was a shot but probably only inconvenienced them more than anything.

CHASING BAD GUYS

Now, back in May, I signed for a set of night vision goggles for some covert, "secret squirrel" operations and had not had an opportunity until the sixteenth to put them to use. There had been times in the past if I was on patrol at night, I would black out and sit somewhere with them on to see if I could observe any illegal activity. Well, this night one of the German officers, Hans Lankes, and I went out and set up near one of the stream crossings into Decani. We sat in the dark under the pine trees, waiting and listening. On a clear, quiet night like that, you could hear things from a mile away. Finally around midnight, I guess, we could hear the clip clop of horses' hooves and the clanking and jangling of the harness and logging chains. Well, finally three subjects passed us, leading a horse cart loaded with logs. Once they passed, we started following them as stealthily as possible. Before we started our little stakeout, we had arranged for one of our vehicle patrols to be ready to assist us. I radioed to the patrol we were following three subjects and to stand by. After we followed them for a while, Hans and I decided to apprehend the suspects. Well, as soon as we yelled "halt," all three bolted, and we were in hot pursuit—okay, at forty-something, maybe my pursuit wasn't so hot, but I was catching up to the slowest one. We were running down a dirt road that was rocky and uneven, so as I was reaching out to collar my man, I stepped into a hole and took a tumble. Well, I rolled and got up running. Okay, so I got up and *tried* to run.

Well, the bad news was all three got away. The good news was we got the horse, cart, and logs. Well, after the adrenaline wore off, my left knee and right elbow were throbbing. After shift I went to my apartment, cleaned up, and went to bed. I was in pain, so I didn't sleep real well. When I got up the next morning, my knee looked like a basketball, was as stiff as a board, and was killing me. My elbow wasn't much better. I ended up having to go to the German KFOR aid station in Prizren which was several miles east of Decani. They didn't do too much for me except X-ray it, tell me I had bad knees, and give me some crutches and some Motrin, which I ate like candy for the next several days. So I guess the lesson in all that was I wasn't cut out to be a James Bond type—more like Maxwell Smart or maybe Inspector Clusoe. Anyway, I hobbled around for a few on crutches until I could limp again on my own.

COMPANY RECRUITER

Now, during all this, "company recruiters" had come to our region—all the regions, in fact—looking for volunteers for Iraq. Well, this was my chance as there were no restrictions; they were looking for live bodies, and mine was alive even if it was a little worse for wear. Jason Hinds and I volunteered. Yes, I broke the first rule I learned in the army again: don't volunteer. Now, before I gave my final word, I had to discuss this with my wife, especially since the security situation in Iraq had drastically changed for the worse. But this was something I still had a real interest and desire to do. Well, of course she gave her support if that's what I wanted. Now, the money in Kosovo was good, we got our monthly paycheck from the "company," and the U.N. gave us a living allowance also. The money in Iraq was much better, in all honesty.

Again, as I said before, it's not just about the money; there are other factors involved in the decision to go to a place like Iraq. So we had to get a cursory exam and blood work to make sure we were still fit. Now, my knee was still pretty stiff and painful at this point, but I saw my opportunity to do this, and it was not and did not stop me. So I signed a new contract for a year tour in Iraq, and I resigned from the U.N. on July 25. Before Jason and I departed, several of the officers at the station threw us a party at a nice little restaurant in Peja. They gave each of us a nice little plaque to commemorate our time in Kosovo. I was on a flight on the twenty-seventh to spend a few days at home. Now, my wife knew I was coming home, but I didn't tell her when. I kept telling her I didn't have a flight yet because I had arranged with some of our friends to pick me up so I could surprise her. My tour had been good overall; I had made some friends and had gotten to do some interesting things even if it wasn't the glamorous event I had envisioned. The U.N. was a real education, to say the least. There were things and people I wouldn't forget, that's for sure.

HOME FOR A SHORT

I arrived home on the twenty-eighth. A friend picked me up at the airport in Jacksonville. He and his wife had arranged to meet my wife for dinner; she had no idea I would be joining her. They had also picked up a dozen roses for me. When we got to the restaurant, I waited until our friends were seated with my wife then I snuck up behind her and whispered in her ear, "Is there room for one more?" Well, she let out a scream, and everyone in the place looked at her like she was crazy. I only had a few days to relax and enjoy myself and to see my new grandson. It was harder than ever to leave this time because of the baby. I admit it was hard to hold back the tears when it came time to say goodbye. I asked myself frequently, *Why am I doing this? Why am I putting myself through this?*

FT. BLISS

I had to report to Bliss on the seventh of August. There were about a dozen of us that had volunteered to leave Kosovo for Iraq; they called us "Kosovo flips." We were at Ft. Bliss for about ten days, training and processing. Now, we "flips" only had to complete the training and processing at Bliss. The rest had already completed two weeks of training in Virginia. It would have been similar to the training prior to the Kosovo mission: firearms, culture, and history, etc. While at Bliss we had to get a thorough medical and dental screening, blood work, HIV and TB tests, vaccinations, etc. You needed to be healthy and able to complete a year tour. Although, some of the people that were passed looked questionable to me—extremely overweight et cetera.

We were fortunate in that the "company" we worked for had a rep there helping and pushing us through the process, including taking care of any issues that came up. He was also pretty good about getting us to the front of the line. If someone needed dental work, he'd get you to a local civilian dentist and get it taken care of. The other civilian contractors were on their own for the most part; at least, they weren't taken care of like we were. Our "company" needed bodies apparently and wanted every one of us to complete the process. We had to get a DOD (Department of Defense) contractor's ID card which would give us access to all military dining facilities, gyms, PX's, et cetera. We also received orders from the State Department saying we were mission essential personnel and entitled access to all military facilities and services, including medical, travel, etc.

We received some training in first aid, chemical and biological warfare, hostage survival, and IED (Improvised Explosive Device) awareness/recognition. Basically, we learned from this that bombs could be anywhere and disguised as anything. That made me feel *much* better. As for the hostage survival class, most of us felt that you had to escape, die trying, or end up on TV or the internet with some animal rambling on about Allah while he sawed your head off with a rusty butcher knife. No thanks. We also had to draw equipment, which meant standing in line for hours. They issued us everything in the world—gas mask, filters, web belt, canteens, cup, cover, body armor, Kevlar helmet with cover, rain gear, sleeping bag, sleeping mat, boots, goggles, gloves, cold gear, etc. Yes, they issued us cold weather gear; there are areas in northern Iraq that are quite cold. While at Bliss, we had the option of living in an army barracks or staying in a local hotel outside the base. That was a hard decision. The only draw back was you had to pay for the room yourself. Now, that wasn't a bad deal because my wife came to visit with me a few days before we flew to Iraq.

HISTORY OF IRAQ

Now, as I have said before, I am by no means a history professor or cultural expert, but I will include a little history of Iraq just to provide some background. The following is my understanding from what I learned from the training and while working in Iraq. I do not claim it to be 100% correct or factual, as I am no expert. Now, obviously Iraq is a predominantly Islamic country, and Iraq, the Islamic faith, and the Middle East are very complex. Here are a few terms related to Iraq: the word *Islam* means submission, *Muslim* means one who submits to God, *Allah* means "the" god, *Jihad* means to struggle or to exhaust one's efforts to please God.

Mohammed, who is the central prophet of Islam, was born around 570 a.d. in what is now Mecca, Saudi Arabia, and died about 632 a.d. According to Mohammed, the archangel Gabriel gave him revelations on which Islam is based, and these revelations are recorded in the Quran. The Old Testament of the Bible tells that Abraham had two sons: the first, Ishmael, who is the father of the Arab peoples, and Isaac, who is the father of Israel or the Hebrew people. Now, it's my understanding that the Muslims believe that Abraham took Ishmael and not Isaac, as the Bible says, up into the mountain to sacrifice at God's command. The Muslims also believe in much of the Old Testament writings such as the creation of man, the great flood, and Moses. They also believe in the final judgment of mankind and Jesus.

Now, they believe that Jesus was a great prophet and man like Mohammed, but he was not divine. Within the Muslim community, I believe there is uncertainty as to whether Christ was crucified and resurrected, as we Christians believe, or whether God took him to heaven alive. I was also told someone was substituted for Christ to be crucified because God would not allow such a prophet to die like this. The main point is they don't believe Jesus is the Son of God or divine, that he was only a prophet. I am a Christian, but I am not a

Bible scholar or world religion expert. So I'm sure someone out there is shooting holes all through this. Again, this is my understanding from conversations I had with Iraqis and from my training.

Mohammed had a daughter, Fatima, who married Ali, and they had two sons, Hasan and Hussain. Hussain was martyred in the battle of Karbala in what is now Iraq. The Shiites believe that the direct descendants of Mohammed are the rightful leaders of Islam, and the Sunnis believe the leadership lies in the hands of the Muslim community at large. This is probably a serious oversimplification of the issue, but it's the main division among the two sects which still breeds hatred and murder today. Iraq or Mesopotamia is mentioned in the Bible and is considered the "cradle of civilization," known for great discoveries in science, mathematics, and astronomy.

Furthermore, Iraq has a long history of violence and coups. Saddam Hussein took power in 1979 and was obviously known for his violent rule. He controlled the country by murder, torture, and intimidation. He was a Sunni and oppressed and exterminated the Shiites and Kurds. In 1990, he invaded Kuwait over border disputes and, probably more realistically, oil rights and revenues. After the first Gulf War and years of unsuccessful sanctions, failed U.N. inspections, and violations of "no fly zones," the U.S. invaded Iraq in 2003.

FLIGHT TO BAGHDAD

Our trip to Iraq was on a commercial plane chartered by the military. Before we flew, we had to load our gear into the belly of the plane. This included duffel bags of all the "stuff" they issued us, plus bags of personal clothing and weapons cases. We would carry Beretta 9mm pistols and M-4 carbines (short version of the M-16 rifle) in either full auto, which fires rounds until you release pressure on the trigger, or three round bursts, which means three rounds are fired every time you squeeze the trigger. Well, they asked for volunteers to load the gear and promised a first-class seat to those that did. Well, I violated the no volunteer rule again. I knew it was going to be a long flight, and first class sounded much better than coach. Well, it took several hours to load the plane, and it was extremely hot, nothing compared to how Iraq would be, though. Well, they really saw us coming because there were no first-class seats, so now I was not only cramped and uncomfortable, I was hot and sweaty. We flew from Bliss to Germany then to Kuwait City. It was a long flight, and between actual flight time and ground time, it took about twenty-four hours. Needless to say, you're pretty worn out when you get there, and the jet lag kicks in, too.

KUWAIT CITY

Once we arrived in Kuwait on the twenty-ninth of August and unloaded our gear, we were met by a "company" rep who had arranged transportation for us and our gear to a hotel. Now, this guy had it pretty good; he was paid well and had an apartment which I believe was paid for, and all he did was arrange for transport for groups coming into Kuwait bound for Iraq. Now, that included arranging to pick us up, get us to a hotel, and then arrange our military flight to Baghdad. I'm not sure what else he did, but it couldn't have been too difficult for the money I'm sure he was making. Now, we stayed in Kuwait for about ten days which wasn't bad since we stayed at a five-star hotel. The rooms were incredible, and every meal was a gourmet buffet. As nice as the hotel room was, I was miserable. The guy I roomed with snored like a freight train. I've never heard anyone snore as loud and long as this guy could. I'd been in the army and reserves for about ten years and had slept in barracks or in the field lots of times with other soldiers, but this guy was incredible. I don't know how his wife had kept from putting a pillow over his face years ago and ending her misery. It's a good thing we really had nothing to do but sit around and wait for our flight because I had to sleep during the day.

Now, Kuwait City is a very nice city—modern hotels, restaurants, and skyscrapers and is known for its world famous architecture. A couple of examples are the Kuwait Towers, which offer an awesome view of the city, and the Persian Gulf. There is also the Grand Mosque. On September 1, we took a short tour around part of the city to visit some of the shops, stores, and other sights. One point of interest we visited was the Kuwait Towers. From the Tower's observation deck, you can see for miles across the gulf, which was placid and turquoise in color. The weather in Kuwait was extremely hot—I think it was around 110 degrees—and very humid and no breeze that I could remember. There were several American-style restaurants such as Kentucky Fried Chicken, Pizza Hut, McDonalds, and I even saw a Starbucks coffee. (I wonder if Mark Lewis knows about that.) We also took a tour of the Kuwait House of National Memorial Museum; it was dedicated to the invasion and eventual liberation of Kuwait. Most Kuwaitis seemed to like Americans for obvious reasons, I guess. Most of the workers at the hotel or any of the stores or shops in town were not Kuwaitis; I saw Filipinos, Pakistanis, Indians, etc. Well, we finally got manifested for a flight to Baghdad, and the vacation was over. We left Kuwait on the sixth of September.

BAGHDAD

We packed up and loaded our gear onto trucks and drove to the U.S. military flight line at the airport. Then we had to unload our equipment, and it was palletized by the military. We had to wait several hours in the heat before our plane was ready and loaded. By this time it was night. We flew on a C-130 (military transport/cargo plane), and if you've never flown on one, they're hot, noisy, and cramped. We sat on a cargo net seat, shoulder to shoulder with body armor and Kevlar helmet and holding your M-4 muzzle down between your knees. You're also required to wear hearing protection, so it's near impossible to hear the instructions given by the flight crew. The flight wasn't too bad altogether and was only about two hours. The bad guys occasionally shoot at military aircraft, so when we landed, the pilot came in hard, fast, and steep—better than most roller coaster rides I've been on.

On the seventh of September, we landed at the Baghdad International Airport (BIAP), which included the commercial airport and the U.S. military flight lines. Actually the "BIAP" is a huge secure complex, housing several different army "FOB's (Forward Operating Bases) such as Camp Victory, Liberty, Stryker, and Dublin. After the plane was unloaded, we gathered up our gear and were met by another "company" rep who welcomed us to Baghdad. We waited for several hours on our escort to take us to a hotel. When our escort arrived, we loaded up about five or six to a vehicle, which were armored Suburbans. Now, crowded wasn't the word for how it felt in those Suburbans. We weren't sitting just shoulder to shoulder; we were just about sitting on each other's laps. I'm pretty tall, and with the Kevlar on, I couldn't sit up straight, and every time we hit a bump, I thought my neck would snap. Now, having been in the military and a road officer for several years, I had been involved in pursuits and off-road driving and thought I was experienced as a driver, but driving through Baghdad was an experience. These guys were good, and it compared to the landing at the airport. All you could do was hold on and pray. Passing on the left and right, over mediums, counterflow (driving against the flow of traffic), and running cars off the road were all in a days work.

As I became more experienced, I learned that this was necessary; if you sat still too long or even moved too slow, you were a potential target. The only thing I can compare it to would be a scene from *Mad Max* or *Road Warrior*. Now, the route or road that leads from the "BIAP" into Baghdad is one of the most dangerous in the world because of the road-side bombs, snipers, and ambushes and was designated "Irish" by the military. All the roads are given a "code" name by the military. Well, we successfully navigated our way to the hotel. When we arrived, we were pretty excited after our Sunday drive through the country. Some of the guys that were further back in the convoy said that they had been fired at during the trip. We were told we should expect a rocket or mortar attack because it always happened when a new group came in.

AL SADEER

We would stay at the Al Sadeer hotel until we received job assignments. The "company" rented two hotels, the Sadeer and the Baghdad. Both were in what was called the "Red Zone" or Indian Territory, so to speak. The "Red Zone" was outside areas secured by our military and considered "safe." Well, we would all learn in due time there was no place in Iraq that was "safe." The "Green Zone" or "International Zone" was the area west of the Tigris River which housed the U.S. Embassy and Iraqi Government. Even though it was called the "Green Zone" and was heavily fortified, it was by no means "safe" either.

Now, I'm sure that the rent for both hotels was probably exorbitant. Besides, the "company" was being paid by the State Department, so just put it on my tab.

The Sadeer was a seven-story brick and concrete building. I'm guessing it was built in the 70s or early 80s, and it looked as if it used to be quite a nice affair in its day. It had a bar, restaurant, laundry, gym, tennis courts, and pool. When we arrived and after unloading our gear, the hotel even had bellmen, I guess you could call them that, to help with our "luggage." During my tour, I went to the Baghdad hotel, which was located on the east side of the Tigris, on a few occasions. It housed the main supply room, arms room, finance, personnel, and—my favorite—the travel section. Travel arranged your flights in and out of country when you went on leave. I always tried to stay friendly with the ladies who worked in that section. I never saw much of the Baghdad other than the lobby and ground floor where the business offices were. It had a pool which looked like some of the swampy areas where I live in Florida; I expected to see crocodiles swimming around in it. The place was a real dump.

After we unloaded our gear and were assigned a room, we had our first real in-country briefing. The briefing was given by the personnel manager; we'll call him "Jack." Jack informed us that this was his show, and he would run it as he saw fit. Now, I thought I had misunderstood the guy until I looked around and saw the expression on everyone else's face. Now, I was thinking, *What a thing to say, considering the apparent need for officers and the obvious desire of the "company" to keep us considering the expense incurred at this point to train and equip us.* This guy was a real character, and it would show even more as you got to know him. I couldn't help but wonder how this guy got this position. I learned he was one of the first in mission and apparently was at the right place at the right time. Rumor has it that he promoted some of his cronies when he got into a position to do so. One of which was eventually demoted due to their lack of ability to handle the position. I also learned later there were very few people who could actually stand the guy and a whole bunch who would have probably killed him if they could have gotten away with it. The briefing was continued, and we were informed that Iraq's a dangerous place, etc. I was fortunate and had a room to myself; it had a bathroom, TV, and a big decent bed. Oh, one more thing I want to mention: you always hear the expression, "It's a small world"; well, sometimes that's so true. Remember the American station commander and operations chief at Decani station in Kosovo? Well, guess who I ran into? I couldn't believe it; it was like old home week down on the farm! Don't get me wrong; at times they were nice guys. I just wanted to keep a respectful distance. I heard months later one or both of them had either left mission on their own accord or had been run off. Not sure which.

SECURITY

The Sadeer was surrounded by a concrete block wall with a metal screen around the top of it. Parts of the wall were supplemented with HESCO barriers. The entrances were further reinforced with concrete barricades. The security force was made up of Americans, South Africans, and a local Iraqi security company. They were all well armed with AK-47s, RPKs, PKCs, and all other devices of death the former Soviet Union had manufactured. There were also guard towers on the roof. The Baghdad hotel was equally fortified, if not more so.

AL SADEER BOMBINGS

Even with the security measures in place, the Al Sadeer was struck by car bombs on two dates. Now, I was not present for either incident but talked to officers who were, but it's hard to describe or understand something like that unless you experienced it. The first occurred on March 9, 2005, a little after 6:00 a.m., so most were preparing for the work day either showering, shaving, checking email, or eating breakfast when the explosion went off. Many spoke of being literally picked up out of bed or whatever they were doing and being thrown against the wall. An explosives-laden garbage truck entered the Ministry of Agriculture compound after shooting and killing one guard. Once inside the compound, the truck detonated, resulting in more Iraqi casualties. The area where it detonated was behind the Sadeer and only protected by HESCO barriers. The results were windows and doors being blown out and numerous Suburbans being destroyed by the blast or ensuing fireball. Dozens of Americans were wounded or injured during the bombing. Someone who was there shared some of the aftermath pictures with me; the crater left by the bomb was huge, several feet in depth and width.

After this attack, concrete barriers were placed completely around the hotel. The next bombing occurred on the twenty-fifth of July, 2005. I saw pictures from both bombings that were taken by an officer who was present and it was devastating. The bombing in March left a huge crater several feet wide and several feet deep. One picture in particular caught my eye because it just seemed so odd. It was a brake shoe from, I would guess the garbage truck, lying on a desk in one of the rooms. The fact it was blown from the vehicle and ended up lying on a desk several stories up is just one of those peculiar things, I guess. The Palestine hotel, which housed western journalists is just down the road from the Sadeer. It was bombed several times resulting in dozens of dead and wounded. Many other hotels around Baghdad were also bombed, resulting in killed and wounded. Now, again I was not present for either incident but was told of the coolness and courage which was displayed in handling the situation and caring for the wounded.

ROOFTOP VIEW OF BAGHDAD

We were allowed to go up on the roof for a look around and to take a few pictures. The view of the city was pretty impressive—the high-rise buildings, palm trees, busy streets full of cars, sidewalks full of pedestrians going about their lives, trying to maintain normalcy in an extreme situation. There are others landmarks of interest visible from the Sadeer rooftop. The Sadeer is not very far from Fardous Square, and the 14th of Ramadan Mosque. Both were made famous on April 9, 2003. Fardous Square is in the center of Baghdad and is where the famous or infamous statue of Saddam Hussein was. It's the one our military hooked up a chain to and then pulled down with one of their armored vehicles. It came to represent our defeat of the Iraqi army and the ousting of Hussein. The Mosque is next to the square, and both were shown over and over on the news. We were instructed in the future to stay off the roof, that it was restricted to security personnel. There was intelligence received on one or two occasions that an attack on the hotel was possibly imminent. Our instructions were to report to our floor commander in full gear in case of an attack. Fortunately this never came to fruition.

STAYING OCCUPIED

Now, we had a few briefings here and there, but most of our time was free. We were taken to the Baghdad Police Academy on the twenty-first, which was several miles from the hotel. We convoyed there to zero our weapons on the rifle range. I occupied my leisure time by going to the gym, reading, watching movies, and staying in touch with my family via email. I mentioned the hotel had a bar, and it opened promptly at 4:00 p.m. daily. There was a lounge area next to the bar with a polished marble floor and chandelier. Now, I'm not a teetotaler and have a drink occasionally and can't judge anyone else who does. But there were a few who were at the bar just about everyday when it opened. Many indulged too much too frequently, which can be a bad thing given the circumstances. Now, the powers that be didn't say too much about it as long as you kept quiet, and unfortunately there were some who couldn't do that.

Now, I will admit that the whole environment was not conducive to pious living. Now, I've been a Christian for many years and maintained my faith, however, not as strongly as I should. I am ashamed to say I wasn't exactly a shining light of Christian living either. I have to guess that those who had a drinking problem probably already had it, and the circumstances there only magnified it. There was also a big screen TV with a satellite dish, so sports were an available diversion. The pool was actually really nice. It was August and still extremely hot, and there's nothing like a cool dip in the pool. The chow was fair; it was prepared by a catering company made up of Indians and Pakistanis. It wasn't that the food was terrible; it was just the same stuff over and over. Friday nights, they put on a decent barbeque with steaks, ribs, baked potatoes, and all the other trimmings that accompany it. The meat was good; I guess it was beef, but it could've been camel, for all I know. They had fresh eggs for breakfast, they had feathers and poop stuck to them, so they must have been fresh. Make mine a three egg omelet. Now, don't get me wrong; I'm not complaining. I took it all in stride and always kept it in my mind that there were guys all over Iraq who had it much worse than I did. I had experienced better and worse in my army career.

RAMBOS

Now, being that I was a "newbie" to the mission, my initial attitude was to sit back, watch, listen, learn, and keep my mouth shut. Now, I was painfully aware of the situation around me, that death or serious injury could be hidden in any trash pile, parked car, or at any overpass, or it could fall down on you in the form of a mortar or rocket. But sometimes I couldn't help but laugh to myself. Now, everyone working as an IPLO (International Police Liaison Officer) was a former or retired cop, and police work is no different than any other profession in that it takes all kinds. Now, I've said before I'm not nor ever was a "high speed" guy. We were not issued a uniform per say. We wore 5.11 tactical gear khakis; some guys did scrounge or buy military fatigues to wear however. Some guys had bought every patch or pin available to have sewn or attached to whatever they might wear—IPLO, CPATT (Civilian Police Assistance Training Team), SWAT, FTO, American flag, their name, etc. There was also an officer at the hotel selling big silver or gold badges. Now, I admit I bought one but never wore it—I sent it home as a souvenir—but many did. I'm not sure what he did other than sell badges, pins, etc. Maybe they recruited him to be the souvenir salesman; I never saw him do anything else. I'm not saying he didn't, but I just don't ever remember seeing it. We were there as mentors and advisors; we had no arrest authority.

Then there were the "Rambos." These were the guys that wore or carried every piece of tactical gear known to man:

Kevlar helmet, tactical ground troop, tactical bullet resistant look-cool-under-any-circumstance Nike glasses, camel back Sahara Desert version hydration system, threat level 10 explosive reactive body armor, tactical vest self loading automatic feed with fifty magazine pouches, grenade smoke multiple color , tactical climbing/rappelling rope nylon 100 ton strength, knife Jim Bowie 200th Anniversary Alamo edition, first aid kit portable field surgical hospital model and boots desert tan kangaroo on meth-amphetamine style. Now, obviously I'm being humorous here, or that's the intention. The point is, some guys went to the point of being ludicrous; they were dragging around more junk than our soldiers. Now, believe me, I wanted my weapons to be the best and functional. I carried all the ammunition I could scrounge, wore as good body armor as I could stand without breaking my back or roasting to death, and I carried the first aid kit I was issued. I wanted to be as safe as possible but also wanted to be able to function. I had to wonder how these guys were going to vacate a disabled vehicle with any speed with all that stuff on. As far as a knife, I carried a pocket knife. Now, you can think what you want, but I had no desire to get into a position where I was going to have to knife fight someone. Maybe they never got to play soldier when they were kids, and this was their chance. Hey, it's your fantasy; be whatever you like, I guess. The reverse of that came during a briefing given by the head armorer (gunsmith); he told us not to modify our weapons and that we didn't need fifty magazines. Well, he was involved in an ambush and apparently everyone involved burned through a large amount of ammunition, so afterwards his opinion changed slightly, I think.

FIRST ASSIGNMENT

Eventually jobs were posted that we could apply for. I put in my paperwork for several, one of which was a training team position. Now, most of us were in general comparably trained or experienced. I had been a trainer in the Army, FTO (Field Training Officer) as a deputy and instructor/firearms instructor qualified, so of course I didn't get that one. I also applied for a position as a Recruiting Coordinator, which I ended up getting. Now, I hoped that this didn't mean going out into Baghdad and actually recruiting cops. I had seen the videos and had no desire to end up in an orange jumpsuit on Al Jazeera TV. Myself, Jason Hinds, who I knew from Kosovo, George Voyles, Terry Jacoby, Jason Barnes, and an officer I'll call "Sam" were all assigned to the Baghdad Police Academy. George Voyles was a Deputy Sergeant in the county when Ruby Ridge, Idaho went down; he was later the sheriff there also. Jason Barnes was a former Marine and Terry Jacoby had already done a tour in Iraq for KBR and had been a site security manager. He shared some pictures with us, and he had already seen some serious stuff. I don't remember much about "Sam" other than we didn't get along too well, which would be an issue later on. I still had the opinion that knowing someone did not hurt your chances of getting a decent posting. Although, the Academy gig turned out to be pretty good overall.

BAGHDAD POLICE ACADEMY

So on about September 22, we packed up our gear again, loaded it into a Suburban, and convoyed to the Academy. As I mentioned before, it's only a few miles' distance, and the trip was short and uneventful. The Academy was the Police College under Hussein. Their officers trained for three years and received a baccalaureate degree in police science. The average police man was not nearly as well trained or educated. The Iraqi police system much more resembled a military organization as opposed to our system. The Academy consisted of several dozen concrete block buildings; many were painted dark or light blue. The Academy dates back to the 1940s, and many of the buildings were in a serious state of disrepair.

The compound overall was dusty, dirty, and there were pools of sewage water from some of the buildings. There were also a large number of palm trees on the grounds, which in August and September, are full of ripening dates. There were crews of men placing canvasses on the ground, and they would climb up the trees to cut the clusters down. I was told Iraq produced some of the best dates in the world. There was some remodeling and renovations going on at the time. Later, a lot of this would be found as substandard and plagued with poor workmanship and corruption. The compound was secured by the U.S. military such as soldiers from the 759th MP Battalion, 89th MP Brigade and others, and the Iraqi Police which I was leery of. The Academy was surrounded by a concrete block wall about ten to twelve feet high. The entrances were fortified with concrete barricades and concertina wire; there were also guard towers around the perimeter complete with .50 caliber machine guns. One such gun tower had the following painted on the wall: "9/11 never forget."

The Iraqi Olympic training center is adjacent to the Academy and is part of the compound. It was known by its U.S. Military name, Camp Provider. Saddam Hussein's son, Uday, was known for raping an untold number of girls and women. In 1995, he had one of his own bodyguards executed for not showing enough "enthusiasm" when torturing Iraqi journalists at the Olympic Committee. He was also notorious for torturing Olympic athletes that didn't perform to his standards. I bet they were beating down the door to join the team. He and his brother, Qusay, were killed in Mosul July 22, 2003, by U.S. forces. Some of the staff we worked with or came into contact with told horror stories of being arrested for some minor infraction, such as not showing enough respect to a motorcade carrying Saddam or one of his sons, then being tortured, beaten or locked in a dog kennel, or other stories of family members picked up by the secret police, never to be seen again. So I can attest that I have spoken to some of the victims of some of Hussein's cruelties. Camp Provider was where the chow hall, PX, laundry, mail room, and barber shop was. Everyone liked getting mail, but I must admit it got to the point where we hated to go to the mail room. The mail sergeant was a strange bird and liked to talk your ear off and wouldn't let you leave. I also remember getting my first haircut there and feeling uncomfortable when the barber broke out the straight razor and started shaving my neck. I couldn't help but think of those horrible beheading videos on the internet.

CAMP SWAMPY

We were housed in a building more like a trailer on steroids. It was a large tin building with a central hallway and ten rooms on either side. The rooms had cheesy fiberboard furniture, armoire, table, and a skimpy little bed. The mattress was several inches too short for me and was about four inches thick; I had a constant backache from it. There were two bathrooms on either side. Each had three tiny little toilet stalls, two sinks, and three showers. The shower nozzle came about to my chest. It was always a mess with dirt, sand, and water on the floor, so it was nicknamed "Camp Swampy." There were two females in the building, so they had it pretty good as far as the shower, but there were around twenty males sharing the one bathroom, so it was a real pain sometimes getting a shower or trying to shave.

One of the females worked for another contractor as an instructor. She was in her late forties or early fifties and at one time was probably a very attractive woman. I don't say that to be mean, only to be honest. Now, I know men go through a "midlife crisis," and I'm not sure what women go through, but whatever it is, I think she was there. I don't mean to make false accusations or impugn her honor, but on numerous occasions, I saw young soldiers leaving her room. Now, maybe they were working on lesson plans, but at 2:00 and 3:00 a.m.? I seriously doubt it.

On more than one occasion, they were pretty loud and apparently intoxicated, which in itself would have been enough to get them at least an Article 15 or maybe a court martial because they were absolutely forbidden to have or consume alcohol. I stepped out into the hallway on one occasion and told her and the soldiers if they were going to have their little late night rendezvous, they needed to keep it to a dull roar. She responded by saying, "We're not doing anything, only talking." *I think thou doth protest too much.* The building itself was surrounded by concrete barriers about eight to ten feet tall, which protected the sides, but the roof was tin and had no cover, so if a rocket or mortar hit it, we were in trouble. We got hit pretty often by indirect fire, so you could either lie in bed and pray a round didn't come through the roof—which I did frequently—or you could run outside to the concrete bunker. Now, the problem with that was I figured if I ran anywhere, I'd run into the next round. Now, believe me, there were times when I was moving at a very brisk walk!

ACADEMY STAFF

Our immediate supervisor was a former cop from Wisconsin, his name was John. His assistant was a female from Alabama or Mississippi—I can't remember which, her name was Trish. They had been there for several months and had started, organized, and were the only IPLOs assigned to the recruiting section until that time. The Academy's commandant was an Iraqi Police Colonel; the coalition representative overseeing the Academy was a British Police Officer. There were about a dozen language assistants and other staff to assist us. I couldn't remember all their names then, much less three years later. I do remember a few names though: "Big" and "Little" Nabil, Majeet, "Gunnie," Hussain, and Jaleel. "Big Nabil" told us he was an Army Captain at one time and was in an anti-aircraft artillery unit. I also remember Jaleel specifically because he was confined to a wheel chair. Under the best of circumstances, I would commend him, but he was working under the worst of situations, so I really respected his drive and willingness to risk his life to help us.

Every one of them was putting themselves at risk, and we could not have accomplished our work without them. Each one of them were good people, and I hope and pray for them and each and every Iraqi that one day there will be peace in their country. There were also three female L.A.s (language assistant), one older and two younger. The elder one made the best chai (tea) and brought in fresh baked flatbread, cheese, and jam every day. I don't know what herb she put in to it, but it gave it almost a mintlike taste, but it wasn't mint leaves. All the males wore western-style clothes such as slacks or jeans; I asked about this and was told most only wore the traditional male Arab robes (dishdasha) at home and to weekly prayers. One of the younger female assistants wore the traditional headdress, a hijab, and jeans on most occasions. The other two always wore the traditional hijab and female robe or dress called an abaya.

SADR CITY

The Academy was very close to Sadr City, home of the Madhi Militia.

Built in 1959 by Prime Minister Abdul Karim Qassim to relieve housing shortages, many poor from outside Baghdad came to live there. It was originally called Al Thawra or Revolution City; under Hussein it was called Saddam City. After Baghdad was occupied by American forces in April 2003, it was renamed Sadr City in honor of Grand Ayatollah

Mohammed Mohammed Sadeq Al Sadr. Under Hussein, Sadr City was the poorest section in Baghdad and the center of Shia resistance to his government.

Muqtadr Al Sadr derives much of his power and prestige from his family. He is the fourth son of Grand Ayatollah Mohammed Mohammed Sadeq Al Sadr, who was assassinated in 1999 along with two of his sons. It was never proven but is suspected Hussein's Baath party was behind it. His father-in-law was Grand Ayatollah Sayyid Mohammed Baqir Al Sadr who was executed in 1980 by Hussein because of his dissent against the Baath Party. Although Al Sadr cannot claim title as a mujtahid (senior religious leader) because he lacks the formal education, he still commands a huge following, including thousands in the Mahdi Militia.

There were combat operations going on constantly, so the sound of gunfire, aircraft, and explosions was a normal thing. I would lay in bed at night, listening to all this and would think someone's getting smoked, and I wouldn't want to be on the receiving end of it because at times it sounded very intense. I would also pray for the safety of our boys going into it.

On occasion an attack at night would be directed at the Academy—gunfire, a few rocket or mortar rounds, then you'd hear the .50 caliber machine guns open up. You could always tell it was a .50 because it has a slower, deeper sound (when it is fired). Then a reaction force would roll out the gate to try and locate and kill the shooters. Rockets made more of a whooshing sound, and the mortar rounds gave off a whistle. The first time I heard one going over, it was pretty scary. Okay, it was scary all the time because you just never knew where it would land or if another one was on the way.

I was never privy to any actual intelligence or security briefing as to what had or was really going on. All the information we got was from the soldiers we worked with. We were told that generally the attacks were originating from Sadr City and the Mahdi Militia. A favorite type of attack would be to place a mortar tube in the back of a pickup truck, stop, lob a few rounds, then leave. It was quick and made it difficult to tell where the attack originated from and to catch those responsible. Of all the rockets and mortars fired at the Academy on a regular basis, there were a few casualties, but I was never made aware of any fatalities. At least not while I was stationed there. Now, I know there were casualties from operations conducted outside the Academy. There were other points of interest close to the Academy. One was the Ministry of Interior (MOI), which was a constant target of mortar and rocket attacks. In fact, I would imagine some of the rounds that hit our compound were meant for the MOI. The other was the Al Shasheed Monument or Martyr's Memorial; it was dedicated to the Iraqi dead from the Iran-Iraq war. It resembles two large blue tear drops. It's clearly visible from the Academy and pretty impressive looking.

RECRUITING COORDINATORS

Now, our job as Recruiting Coordinators consisted of processing potential police candidates. Every day except Friday, which is the Muslim day of prayer, we received a list or manifest of names from the MOI. The list of names came from the different areas in the Baghdad region, generally one group from one area at a time. I'm not completely sure how this process worked, other than the MOI would make a request for bodies from the local government, municipality or whatever. A lot or most of the time the local sheiks became involved in the selection of names which probably resulted in a degree of favoritism and/or corruption. The lists ultimately had to be approved by the MOI, so again, I would imagine there was a degree of corruption at that level also. In fact, at that time and probably still today, the whole Iraqi government, police, and military were rife with corruption. When the C.P.A. (Coalition Provisional Authority) turned over control in June of 2004, I believe it was pretty apparent that due to corruption and other factors, the Iraqi government was not ready to take over. Unfortunately politics and common sense did not prevail.

Our military would also prep groups and send them to us. Obviously when we processed a group such as this, they were generally good to go, and most if not all would pass the screening process. We normally processed around one hundred daily—generally less, sometimes more. On Thursdays, female applicants were allowed to come and be processed, and we'd have around a dozen. Iraq was trying its best to be an equal opportunity employer. Before this system, it was my understanding that persons interested in being police officers would show up at the Academy, and as many could be taken were allowed in. The MPs told me things got out of hand on numerous occasions, and near riots ensued. On one specific occasion, shots had to be fired, resulting in casualties.

PROCESSING APPLICANTS

There were several steps in processing the candidates. Every morning we went to the office to get the daily manifest. Then we went to the back gate of the Academy, which was by Palestine Street, where out language assistants would meet us. From Palestine Street, you could clearly see The Martyr's Monument to the east. Every morning there would be dozens—sometimes well over one hundred—potential applicants waiting. The candidates had to have a valid identification and be from eighteen to thirty-five years old. Usually one or two of us would work with an L.A. to check each candidate's ID to the manifest. The fact we didn't read or speak Arabic was enough of a problem, but another thing that was a little confusing were Arabic names; not if you're Arabic, but for a dumb Florida boy like me, it was. Arab names are lengthy. For example, a man's name might be Ali bin Ahmed bin Saleh Al-Fulani, meaning Ali son of Ahmed son of Saleh of the Al-Fulani family. And we learned quickly never to just call out Ali, Ahmed, or Mohammed because you'd usually have ten guys come forward. You always called out at least two or three of the person's name. My pronunciation was pretty poor also and usually got some good laughs. There were always several in the group who didn't bring their ID or had lost it, so we'd tell them to come back on a particular day, and we would process them. Many of the candidates either looked too young or too old, but their ID indicated they fell within the age range. Also many of the ones who had to return on a later day had questionable IDs. I'm sure many of them had fake IDs, but all we could do was rely on our language assistants to translate as best they could. However, they would on occasion tell us that they thought a guy's ID was questionable.

The back gate of the Academy was generally extremely busy every morning. Hundreds of people wanted access to the compound including police applicants, workers and Academy staff. Each one had to be searched before entering. One thing that made me nervous—and I'm sure it would be an understatement to say everyone else, for that matter—was the fact that the Academy was a prime target for a car bomb or suicide bomber. It would have been easy pickings with dozens or hundreds lined up waiting to come in. I thank God we never had that happen while I was there.

There was a car bomb that went off on Palestine Street in September or October—I can't remember the specific day. There were so many explosions on a daily basis all over Baghdad that we could hear. I remember it because some of the debris actually landed inside the Academy compound. We were told later that a car had tried to pass a security checkpoint leading to the Academy and was fired on, causing it to detonate. I know there were casualties but don't know the exact number. On December 6, 2005, two suicide bombers were able to enter the Academy and detonate, killing over forty and wounding scores more. I was not present for that horrific event, but during my second Iraq tour, I met a guy who was. He told me about it and shared some pictures. Pretty gruesome stuff; bodies literally shredded, bodies dismembered, and some completely intact but crushed internally from the immense shock wave from the blast. Everyone would be searched by the MPs and Iraqi Police on duty. After the candidates were checked on the roster, we would search them again as an extra precaution, line them up, and march them to a small classroom. On several occasions, we ventured out onto Palestine Street to help the military clear out large crowds still lingering and trying to get into the Academy.

FIRST STEP

The next step was a very simple literacy test to see if they had basic Arabic reading and writing skills. The test consisted of reading a short paragraph and answering ten questions. They were required to answer six correctly. Next, they were required to complete an application, which was similar to one you or I would fill out for a job. Each applicant had to complete a form indicating he had never been a Baath Party member. If an applicant had been a member, they were required to complete a form renouncing their affiliation or membership. As far as their application or Baath party association, we had no way to verify any of the information. Next, was a simple physical agility test consisting of a few push-ups, sit-ups, and a short obstacle course. The candidates were given a cursory medical exam. If they had a pulse and were walking around, they were good to go. This is a slight exaggeration, but the doctor would call five or ten into the room at one time and ask them a few questions as to their medical condition, and I don't remember too many being turned away for medical reasons. So you be the judge.

The last step was an oral interview with the Academy commandant or others from his staff. Sometimes the Colonel would ask the candidate to read or write something to further ascertain their literacy skills. Now, the worst part of this job was having to tell someone that they had failed a portion of the process and had to leave. I had numerous people literally cry and beg not to be made to leave and give them another chance. It was really tough when a female would tell how her husband was dead and she had children to feed. I wanted to help, but more often than not, I was helpless to do anything. It was difficult to explain there was nothing I could do for them because they looked at Americans as being able to do or change anything. It was hard to explain that I was only a peon with no authority to make such decisions. On occasion the only thing we could do was help someone get a position as a language assistant if they were fluent in English. If a candidate passed everything, they were given a letter with a date to report for an Academy class.

JORDAN OR BAGHDAD

The Academy was eight weeks in length. I was not an instructor so cannot vouch for the type or quality of training; it was conducted by U.S military personnel and American instructors from a company called MPRI. I know that it consisted basically of Iraqi law, human rights, and firearms. The candidates we processed went to either the Baghdad or Jordan Academy. There were other Academies around Iraq also. At the Baghdad Academy, there were about 1,000 recruits attending each class and the goal was to double that. As I said, remodeling, renovation, and construction was ongoing while I was there. Now, things all over Baghdad were bad— lack of water, electricity, sewage service, etc. The Academy was no different; water for our showers was trucked in, power was provided by generators which had to be maintained, and septic tanks had to be periodically pumped out. It was a cumbersome system, and my hat is off to all the people who did all that to make things run as smoothly at the Academy as possible.

Overall, living conditions at the Baghdad Academy were primitive in addition to the security situation. The Academy in Jordan I can only assume would be much more desirable. The facility itself would have to be light-years ahead of Baghdad, plus no one was trying to kill you every day. The number sent to each was dictated to us by higher-ups. Most of our candidates stayed in Baghdad, but on several occasions, we had to prepare a group for Jordan. This required giving all the candidates a report date and when they arrived again, checking their ID against our roster. Then they were searched, their baggage was checked by K-9s, and they were loaded onto a bus and escorted to the BIAP by the military.

Other recruits were sent directly to Jordan or Baghdad from the respective regions. Most of the candidates were willing to go to Jordan for the above stated reasons; some, however, refused to go because they couldn't leave their families for two months, which is understandable. As I understood it, if they went to Jordan, they stayed until they completed or washed out. There were no holidays or breaks. On the flip side of that, some would flat-out refuse to stay in Baghdad because of the security situation and the risk to their lives. If they wanted to be a cop, the Academy was only the beginning of the risk they were taking. Now, I said before that the Jordan Academy would seemingly be more desirable. I heard of at least one incident where recruits basically rioted in Jordan because they felt the discipline imposed by the western instructors was too harsh. One issue that I never understood was groups were being sent back from Jordan with no military or other security escort. Some of those groups were like lambs to the slaughter—ambushed, kidnapped, executed, and/or beheaded. Every time I heard about such an incident on the news, I just had to scratch my head and ask why.

THINGS ARE GETTING HOT

At the time, things were really heating up all over Iraq, and attacks against coalition and Iraqi forces were increasing daily. Police checkpoints were being car bombed, police patrols were being ambushed, police stations were being overrun, policemen and military were being kidnapped and brutally murdered by animals claiming to do the will of Allah. I talked to many of the candidates, and some seemed to want to make a difference and be a part of the rebuilding of their country. Others told me flat-out the police or military were the only jobs available and they had families to support. Either way I give them credit for doing it because, regardless of the motivation, it took guts. I couldn't help but look at each group as not much more than cannon fodder or grist for the mill. But I also figured it was their country, and if our servicemen/women, contractors and advisors such as myself, and the others I worked with were willing to risk life and limb, they should be, too. You can only truly appreciate freedom if you've given something, sacrificed something to achieve it. In all fairness, I guess Iraqis from all walks of life have sacrificed and given their blood, and hopefully God in heaven will bless them one day with peace and security, at least as much is possible in the world we live in.

SAME OLD SAME OLD

Now, there wasn't anything really exciting, sexy, or glamorous as a Recruiting Coordinator. It was pretty much the same routine everyday: get up 0500, eat chow at 0600, go to office and get manifest at 0700, back gate at 0730, process candidates and at 1200 rotate everyone to lunch, and finally finish candidates at 1600. Day in and day out was the same, unless we had to process a group for Jordan, which provided a slight change from the norm. I have to admit that overall, in spite of the mortar and rocket attacks, the Academy was a relatively "safe" place to be. For all the rounds fired, it's a miracle the casualties weren't higher. Going outside the wire was the really dangerous place to be. At the back gate where we worked, there was an old metal basketball gymnasium that we utilized from time to time. It was a typical gym, I guess. It was a grayish metal with green trim and rust spots here and there. The inside was pretty run down; the bleacher seats, which were green plastic, were still there; yellow metal railing and a scoreboard was still up along with the Olympic rings. The court itself was dirty, and some of the rooms attached were knee-deep in trash in some places.

On the twenty-seventh of September, we had a fairly close call; I guess you'd call it a close call. We had just left the gym a few minutes before when several mortar rounds hit the back gate area. One went right through the roof of the gym, leaving a large hole several feet in diameter. Pieces of metal roofing, insulation, and AC ductwork were scattered on the floor. We also were able to collect several large pieces of shrapnel from the round. If we were still there with the group of candidates, there's no telling how many casualties there might have been. It's one of those moments where you look at each other and go, "Whew! That could have been ugly." I remember one attack when George and I got caught in the open; it's one of those situations where you're not sure whether to walk, run, or just stand still and pray for the best. We ended up ducking into the nearest bunker we could find.

PHOTO SECTION

Serbian Monastery covered in snow.

The view taken from my apartment looking northwest
toward the Prokletijie mountain range.

Another view from my apartment looking
west towards the mountains.

Another view looking west from my apartment with the
mountains shrouded in snow and fog.

Me on a "Kosovo Harley".

Me standing in front of a U.N. "Coca Cola" at Junik
station in the Decani area.

Decani police station.

Protestors marching through Decani during riots 17-19
March 2004.

War memorial at Gllogjan.

Celebration at Gllogjan war memorial March 4, 2004.

Chalets at Camp Rugova Rugova pass outside Peja

Gorge through Rugova pass with stone bridge.

Shroud of clouds around mountains by Decani.

Mark Williams and I outside Camp Rusty.

Making a friend at Bab Al Sheikh police station.

Standing in a guard tower overloooking the street outside
Bab Al Sheikh police station Baghdad.

Mark Williams, myself and members of the 2nd Platoon
1st squad 118th MP Co. Airborne at Bab Al Sheikh
police station.

Mark and I at Bab Al Sheikh police station showing off
our "big guns".

Effects of an "EFP" (explosive formed projectile)
on our HUMVEE.

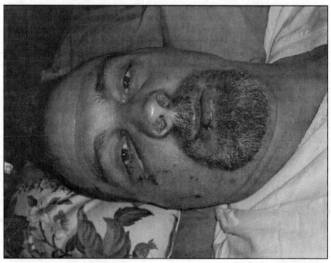

Landstuhl Army hospital shrapnel wounds to the face.

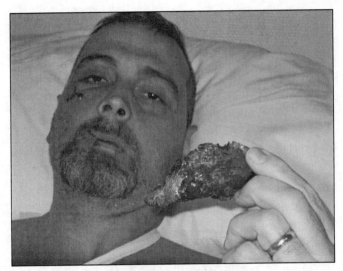

Landstuhl Army hospital piece of
shrapnel taken from my back.

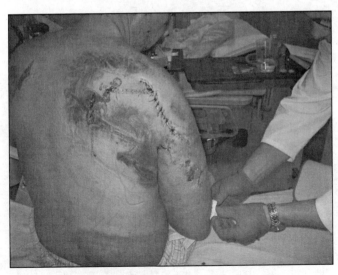

Shrapnel wounds to my back, arm and shoulder
"Yosemite Sam took a lickin'".

THE "DOC"

The literacy test we were administering when I first arrived was very basic as I first described. Not able to read Arabic, we had to rely on our interpreters, and according to them, the test was designed to ascertain if the candidates had a very rudimentary comprehension of the language and basic writing skills. Around the end of September and beginning of October, the "Doc" and his assistants came to the Academy to evaluate a new literacy test. The "Doc" was a Ph.D. and had designed tests for police departments in the states to test officers' literacy, comprehension, and reasoning skills. I'm not sure who he knew in the Department of Defense or Department of State to get this gig, but he had to know someone. If he could evaluate and prove his test, he would get the rights, I guess, to have his test administered to all police candidates in all of Iraq. I'm sure it would have to mean quite a bit of money in his pocket at some point in time.

The "Doc" was very secretive and guarded as to the contents of the test. I could understand the necessity to guard from the possibility of it being copied and possibly sold to potential candidates. But sometimes it seemed when we asked questions about it, he was a little too secretive. We had to ask the L.A.s to tell us what it contained because when it was administered, they obviously had to give instructions to the candidates taking it. Each test booklet and answer sheet were numbered, counted, and accounted for before, during, and after each test session. The test booklets and answer sheets were otherwise under lock and key. It was a very complex test consisting of several hundred questions testing one's ability to read, reason, and comprehend. It was one of those bubble in the answer with a number two pencil deals, which had to be graded in a special scanner. It took several hours to complete. Each person's test was graded on some kind of percentage curve, which was compared to all the other candidates tested. Don't ask me; it was all very complicated. It wasn't a matter of the person scoring 70% or whatever out of a hundred.

The original test was simpler and much easier to understand. I couldn't help but feel this whole thing was a little too complicated for most of the candidates being tested, most of whom had very little education. I understand the need and desire to select the very best candidates, but the complexity of it seemed advanced for even some police agencies in America. I felt the real answer was in basic education, but that was an issue that had to be addressed at the governmental level and would take years to effect any changes. Anyway, some of the candidates scored quite high, and some scored quite low. I asked the "Doc" what the chance would be of someone passing the test just by bubbling in the dots at random—sort of the same method I used on most of my high school tests. He told me the chances were very slim; however, there were several who "passed" the test but would be washed out after the oral interview with the colonel because they could not read and write satisfactorily. We brought this to the "Doc's" attention who told us to inform him every time this occurred, so he could keep track. I suppose this was all very scientific and in the end would work for the best for choosing acceptable candidates.

DOC'S ASSISTANTS

"Doc" had two assistants; one was a retired appellate judge from Alabama or Mississippi. There was also a female who was their clerical assistant. She was a very nice lady in her forties who I talked with on a few occasions. She had grandchildren, and I couldn't help but ask what in the world she was doing there. I didn't mean any disrespect because that was a question I asked myself on occasion. I just was curious why she would risk life and limb to be there. She told me she was from a small town and wanted to do something different and exciting.

As I said, "Doc" was a Ph.D., but I really had to question his common sense. When he and his crew first arrived in Baghdad, they were living in a hotel in the "red zone." No security, no nothing. They were just hanging out at the hotel, eating in the restaurant, and he had hired a driver, a guy he didn't know from Adam. He was putting their lives in serious jeopardy. It would be too easy for this guy to drive them anywhere and hand them over to the highest bidder. When I found out about this, I asked him what he was doing. He asked me if I really thought this was a bad idea. I told him "bad idea" didn't begin to describe what I thought. I asked him if he had any idea what was going on out there and if he had any inkling of the potential danger. He said, "You know, I really hadn't given it much thought" or words to that effect. About the next day or so, he and his crew were living at the Academy. I have to confess I was relieved because they were nice people, and I would hate to think something would happen to any of them because of one person's poor judgment or failure to grasp the real-world situation.

On the twenty-ninth of October, we were invited to have dinner by one of the lieutenants on the Academy staff. I don't remember his name, and I really didn't know him. Anyway, he had invited us to have dinner, which he brought to the Academy; it consisted of roast chicken, bread, and vegetables. It was very good and was a welcome break to eat something other than chow hall food. Don't get me wrong; generally dining hall food was excellent. KBR ran the DFAC (Dining Facility) and has received a lot of bad press about corruption and excessive billing, but the chow halls were good. They were always clean, and the food was abundant and well prepared. It beat eating MRE's (Meal Ready-to-Eat) any day of the week. Now, this guy was at first nice, then weird, and then just plain scary. He seemed to take a liking to Jason, and I mean a real liking, as in he talked about making him his wife. Now, I don't know if this guy was just joking around or serious. If he was joking, he had us all fooled. Now, poor Jason didn't know what to do; he comes from a smaller town in Texas, and if some guy had done that back home, Jason would have knocked the guy's lights out, as I would. I think Jason was trying really hard to be gracious and take it hopefully as a joke. Finally he had to tell the guy to cut it out or else. It made us all feel uncomfortable, and we asked John what was up with that. John told us he had no idea what the guy's problem was and was sorry for getting us into the situation. He figured it was just dinner and didn't have any inkling this guy was a nutcase. Fortunately I don't remember seeing that lieutenant too much after that and got no more dinner invitations.

I said the chicken was good, and it was, but for about two weeks after that, I hated life. I was so sick and spent most of the time in bed or in the bathroom. It was strange because I was the only one; no one else was affected. I went to the medics and got some medicine, but it hung on for days. Now, one humorous incident—I guess you could call it humorous—I said I was sick, and I don't mean to be gross or rude, but I was indisposed in the bathroom. Well, wouldn't you know, the bad guys would figure it was a good time to start lobbing mortar rounds. Well, what do you do, possibly embarrass yourself, or possibly get yourself killed? I remember thinking, *Man what a compromising position to be caught in or get killed in.*

Now, everyone likes to find a way that suits him or her to keep occupied during any free time. I spent time reading, working out, watching movies, or communicating with the family. When it worked, we had the internet in our rooms. When it didn't, there was a Phone Center on Camp Provider which catered to the soldiers. It had phones, internet, video games, cold drinks, candy, etc. Amazingly, it burned down on the thirtieth; I heard the cause was an electrical short. Now, if you could have seen some of the electrical boxes in most of the buildings, it's amazing the whole place didn't burn down. An electrical inspector here in the states would have a fit. So I know many a soldier was bummed until the place was rebuilt a month or so later. I'm sure the proprietors had been making a tidy profit and were anxious to get back into business. On Halloween several of the soldiers came around dressed in traditional Arab garb, complete with shemagh (head covering) and dishdasha (robe), and came around our barracks "trick or treating." It was their way of breaking up the monotony and having some fun.

DETAINEES

Like I said, attacks directed at the Academy were fairly frequent if not all that intense. Thankfully, most of the time, they were more of a nuisance than anything. There was a small detention area on the Camp cordoned off with concertina wire, and from time to time, there would be a few subjects handcuffed and blindfolded there. Wonder if any of them were important enough to ship to Gitmo for a friendly chat session?

COMMANDO UNIT

From about the twentieth of November through the middle or so of December, there was a Police Commando Unit from the Basra area at the Academy training. They wore blue urban style fatigues and a red beret that looked too small for their heads. It looked like a small pizza pan or something on their heads. Some of them looked pretty tough and professional. We took an opportunity to speak with some of them and, of course, take some photos. I felt bad for these guys because they had stuck them in some vacant barracks with no real support. I don't know how they were showering or what toilet facilities they had available. I've already described the primitive conditions at the Academy. I saw some of them washing off with a towel and bottled water and hanging their laundry outside to dry on makeshift clotheslines. Now, it was pretty cold in November and December, so they were roughing it.

Many of them were not prepared and definitely not dressed for cold weather with no jackets, gloves, or even socks. Several of us gathered up what we could—some socks, gloves, thermal underwear, etc. We had every intention of doing a good thing; little did we know what it would open us up to. We were hounded almost daily by these guys asking us for stuff, and no matter how many times we would tell them we had nothing else to give, they would still ask. I did manage to get a couple of cool shoulder patches from a couple of them. On the fourteenth of December, a couple of the barracks they were in went up in flames. Not sure what the cause was—accidental, electrical, or maybe an attempt to get better living conditions—not that there was much better. It's kind of funny; the L.A.s were the same way. I had my wife send a package with some college football hats, scarves for the females, and some other stuff to give out. Well, after I gave out the hats, you'd have thought I was giving away gold. They all wanted one and one for their kids, buddies, etc. After my wife sent me two or three more boxes full of hats, I had to cut it off before I went broke providing head gear for all of Baghdad.

THANKSGIVING

Thanksgiving 2004 was pretty nice considering being 10,000 miles from home. The DFAC was all decked out in decorations, including a dragon sculpted out of what looked like crab leg shells. Still haven't figured out what a dragon had to do with Thanksgiving, but it was cool looking. Dinner was the traditional turkey with all the trimmings, including bottles of sparkling grape juice on all the tables. It was really good. They really took care of our troops, and they deserved everything they could get to make their lives a little more comfortable.

TROUBLE IN PARADISE

Our supervisor never interfered or questioned how we ran the back gate as long as we got the candidates properly processed. The only time we generally saw him and his assistant was when we had a Jordan group to process because it took all available hands to get it done. The four of us, Jason Hinds, Jason Barnes, George Voyles, and I, had developed a system by this time. "Sam" had long ago decided he didn't want to be part of our team. We arrived in August, so it was pretty hot processing the people at the back gate. After about a week, he decided it wasn't for him, so he started hanging around the office with our supervisor and his assistant to be their gopher or whatever. I'm not sure if it was the heat, the potential danger of a suicide bomber, the random mortar attacks, or if he was just lazy. We devised a system to give each member of the team a break. Once all the police applicants were in the classroom and the literacy testing was well underway, one or maybe two of us could cut out early around lunchtime. We took turns leaving early if the situation allowed it. Now, I'm not sure if anyone specifically told our boss what we were doing. I personally didn't, but we were getting the job done, and no one ever questioned our method, so I figured it was no problem.

Well, the boss had to go on sick leave and left his assistant in charge, who found out how we were running things. I wonder who told her. It's not that we were hiding anything, and she was in charge at the time, and so if she disapproved, no problem; we'd stop. Well, if she'd approached it in a different manner, everything would have been okay. She started accusing us of being lazy and goofing off and that she was in charge and we'd do what she said, and if we didn't like it, we could leave. She said she was sick of how we did things. She told us that soldiers and some of the instructors living in our building had complained about us lying around the barracks all day. She also threatened to get us fired. Well, we knew that wasn't true because we weren't lying around the barracks, and we were getting our work done, and no soldiers were in our barracks to know if we were or weren't lying around all day unless they were there "preparing lesson plans" with the female at the end of the hall, which they had no business doing.

Well, we ended up having a meeting with the head, Brit. We flat-out asked him if he had any problems with our work or if any complaints had been received on us. He said he had received no complaints and had no problem with our work. We knew right then that she was on a power trip. Well, unfortunately the working atmosphere was shot after that. Jason was having some personal issues back home and ended up leaving. It was the straw that broke the camels back for him. This was a real shame because he was a good guy, and I enjoyed working with him. Terry Jacoby also ended up leaving shortly after all this went down; another good guy with good experience.

One time after that, "Sam" came to the classroom and had something to say about how we were doing things. I told him that he was not in charge of us, and since he never came to the classroom to help, his opinion was not really needed.

Some other things were said, and I got pretty hot and started towards him, but George grabbed me by the arm and held me back. I was mad but not sure what I would have done if George hadn't been there. Anyway, "Sam" filed a complaint against me that I had threatened him. Most of the time, it seemed he was chasing after a young girl who was the niece, I believe, of one of our L.A.s. She was young and attractive, and this guy was in his fifties and talking about how he was going to marry her. He complained on me one or two other times afterwards for looking at him wrong. Now, I did all I could to avoid the guy because I didn't want to get in trouble or fired. One night he came up to me in the barracks, telling me I needed to move from one room to another to double up with someone else. Now, at this point, I'm ashamed to say I went off on the guy. I didn't curse or anything. At least, I hope I didn't, but I told him that he had no authority over me, which he did not, and that he needed to mind his own business, and if I needed to do something, someone actually in authority over me could tell me. I venture to say when I told him this, I probably was not using my inside voice.

"JACK'S" CRONIE COMES TO VISIT

Now, as I just said, "Sam" had filed some complaints against me with personnel. "Jack," the personnel manager at the Al Sadeer, sent one of his cronies to the Academy to "investigate" the complaints "Sam" had made against me. "Lance" interviewed me, and I freely admitted that I didn't get along with the guy, but as long as he left me alone and didn't try to act like he had authority over me, I would continue to do my job. I told him the other reasons I had issues with the guy was he didn't want to do any work—at least not as described in our specific job title, or in any other capacity that I was aware of. He had specifically claimed that I had threatened him in the presence of George Voyles. Now, that was totally untrue, and George did in fact attest to that. I told "Lance" he could interview the others, and I thought he would find all the others would agree with me. Once again I told him that I was not without fault in the situation, but I was trying to do my job to the best of my abilities. Well, "Lance" left me and spoke to me again a few hours later and told me he had spoken to the others. He told me not to worry, that in his opinion the complaints were groundless, and I had nothing to worry about. Well, I should have seen the train that was coming down the track on this one. Well, fortunately our supervisor came back, and we told him what had happened, and things returned to somewhat normal, but to me it was never the same.

TRAVELING

I left the Academy in the middle of December for Christmas leave. The day before I left, I got to move my gear into a building across from our barracks that had been under renovation. It was a concrete block structure and maybe offered a little more protection than the tin can we were living in. The day I left Baghdad was crazy as far as the weather; it was cold with rain, then some sleet, and some snow flurries. I'd never pictured that. I was looking forward to a break from everything and to seeing my family. Now, traveling out of Iraq was an almost monumental task. When you took leave or C.T.O. (Compensatory Time Off), you had to put in a request, and it had to go through your chain of command for approval.

Only a certain number were allowed on leave from your particular job assignment, and this depended on the total number assigned. After you submitted a leave request, it had to be approved by your supervisor; then it was sent to the travel section at the Baghdad hotel. The travel section would then arrange your flights for you or if you wanted you could go online and see what flights you preferred. You could then submit your itinerary to travel because they purchased your tickets etc. So then you had to get transportation from your job location to the Sadeer, where you would usually stay for a day or two until your flight out. Transportation in these situations was handled by the "movement control team." This was a group of officers whose main duty was to provide transportation to and from the Baghdad airport and points in between for officers such as myself. However, there was a group of American officers that conducted K-9 training at the Academy that lived at the Sadeer Hotel. I was lucky and hooked up with them for a ride. Then the "movement control team" would take you to the Baghdad hotel in a convoy of several vehicles where you had to pick up your ticket out of Baghdad.

Now, remember this is Baghdad, so any time you traveled, it wasn't a Sunday drive; you were in full gear, armed and always expecting something very bad to happen, but as for me, I was always praying nothing would. The movement control team was on the road several times a day, every day of the week traveling on "Route Irish," which was the military designation for the road to the BIAP. It was at one time the most dangerous road in Iraq—in the world, for that matter. Then you flew out of Baghdad on either Jordanian

Air, which I preferred, or Iraqi Air. Now, you know why I preferred the former.

Iraqi Air never instilled much confidence in me. The planes were old, and I have no idea how well maintained they were. Although, if I remember correctly, the flight from Baghdad to Amman was about $900 because of the danger involved to the flight crews. The pilots had to fly pretty aggressively coming into or leaving Baghdad—as evasively and aggressively as a commercial airliner can anyway. Every time I flew out, I went through Amman Jordan and was met by a "company" representative. This person was usually a local who got you through customs. If you were staying overnight, you had to get a temporary visa to stay in Amman. If your flight was leaving in a few hours, the rep gave you your tickets, and you waited on your flight. If you were staying overnight, you were taken to the Sheraton Hotel to get a room and your tickets home. The Sheraton was a very nice place, and generally I was able to relax some compared to being in Iraq. Considering Jordan is a Muslim country and bad things have happened there, I never felt 100% comfortable and always tried to stay on my guard. From there I usually flew through Germany or France then to the U.S. After it was all said and done, it was quite a long ordeal, and I was usually exhausted once I actually arrived home.

CHRISTMAS LEAVE

As always, it was enjoyable to be home, see your family, hold your wife close, hug your kids, sleep in a comfortable bed, take a nice hot shower without having to hunch down, and to eat a home-cooked meal. Iraq was a bit stressful, so every time during this tour that I went home, I was never able to completely unwind. I tried not to do it, but subconsciously I found myself counting down the days until I had to return. I tried to put it out of my mind, but it was difficult. Christmas was good; it was my grandson's first. Obviously since he was only about five months old, he wasn't really aware of what was happening. The days flew by, and the time came to leave, which as usual was excruciatingly difficult.

RETURNED TO BAGHDAD

I returned to Baghdad on the seventh of January, which would turn out to be a day of "infamy" for me. I stayed overnight until I could get transportation back to the Academy. I was looking forward to getting settled in to my new room in the freshly renovated building. It promised to be more comfortable than the tin can we lived in. I also wanted to get back to work. I was able to hitch a ride the next morning with the K-9 instructors going to the Academy to teach the I.P. (Iraqi Police) K-9 handlers.

The ride over was uneventful, and as I got out of the vehicle the I.P.L.O. in charge of the instructors told me they were only staying for a few hours, and I was to have all my stuff packed and be ready to go. I asked him what he was talking about. He told me I had been transferred. I told him he didn't know what he was talking about and he must have the wrong guy. He said, "You're William Little, right?"

"Yes," I said.

He said, "Well, you've been transferred, and go pack your gear."

I asked him who told him this, and he said "Jack," then it was all clear to me. I knew this was because of "Sam," and all the stuff "Lance" had fed me was baloney. I went to talk to my boss to see what was going on. He said "Jack" had informed him I was transferred when I was on leave. He asked me if anyone had told me. I said "No, not a word." He then told me "Jack" should have told me, and this was wrong, but there was nothing he could do.

Now, I didn't want to be transferred because the Academy was a decent job. I felt like I was doing a little something, and yes, I admit it was relatively safe. It's not so much that I was being moved but how it all transpired. "Jack" had really shown his true colors, how he was a conniving power-hungry egotist. When I came back from leave, I had seen the guy several times at the Sadeer, and he never said a word. I had stood next to his desk while I was getting a room for the night; he heard me give the person my name, and he didn't say a word. Instead of packing my stuff at the Sadeer and dragging it to the Academy and dragging it back again, I could have left it there. That guy was a piece of work. Well, what could I do but pack my stuff and try to say goodbye to the others? It always seems when there's a good thing going or something is working, something or someone has to ruin it.

ASSIGNMENT: SADEER

Well, I was taken back to the Sadeer. I unloaded my gear, left it in the lobby, and went to the personnel office to find out what was going on. Well, guess who was sitting at his desk? You guessed it! My buddy "Jack." Well, I was pretty upset at this point, so I was pretty blunt with the guy, demanding to know what was going on and why I hadn't been told I was being transferred. Well, of course he fired back, "Don't come in my office telling me what to do and how to do my job!"

I shot back, "I'm not telling you your job. I just want to know what's going on! It didn't make sense dragging my gear all over Baghdad when I could have left it here!" Then I asked where I was being transferred to. He told me he hadn't decided yet. So this was definitely not about mission needs; this was him with an axe to grind. So I spent the next several days doing busy work, shredding and filing documents, moving furniture and equipment. There was another guy there, sharing the burden of "Jack's" wrath. He had apparently butted heads and lost, too. I was really angry and was seriously considering telling him off and going home. Then I thought, *Why let this egocentric moron ruin your mission? It's not about him but what you hoped to accomplish and be a part of.* So I sucked it up and kept my mouth shut.

MOVEMENT CONTROL

After a few days, I was temporarily assigned to the movement control team. Again, their main function was as a glorified armored taxi service. Don't get me wrong; it was a necessary function. All the guys were good to work with. The team leader was a good guy. He was former military and SWAT guy from South Carolina. "1ˢᵗ Sergeant" was retired army and former cop. There was a guy from Atlanta and a young female from Key West to name a few of them. Like I said before, moving anywhere in Baghdad was no joke. You were geared up and ready for anything at any time. It was an interesting experience, and the short time I did it, I learned a lot. I was the new guy and less experienced, so I either rode as a gunner in the back seat or sometimes "shotgun" in the front passenger seat. We always traveled in a convoy of at least three armored Suburbans. Each vehicle was supposed to have at least three occupants: the driver, the "shotgun" position to watch the right side of the vehicle, and one behind the driver to watch the left side of the vehicle. The driver's job was to drive and nothing else. Four or more was best because then you had better 360-degree coverage.

When the mission first started, all the SUVs were "soft skins" or unarmored. After things started getting crazy, the "company" started buying vehicles that were armored from the "factory" or added armor to them. The doors weighed about a hundred pounds, and the bullet-resistant glass on all the windows was about two inches thick. Some of the vehicles had a machine gunner in the rear; he basically sat in a metal box with an opening to the rear so he could keep security on the vehicle's "six" or six o'clock position. Traffic in Baghdad was quite heavy, and maneuvering through it was an art. One thing that made travel in Baghdad a nightmare—other than the crazy American contractors, military, and car bombs—was the fact all the traffic lights were out. I'm sure those are on the long list of things to do: working government, defeat insurgency, electricity, water, sewage, and—oh yes—traffic lights.

There were traffic cops at most major intersections, which we generally ignored. All in all, it was an uneventful experience. Nothing major happened; no roadside bombs, no ambushes, nothing. Other than running a few cars off the road or having to ram a couple others, it was no big deal. We ran several missions a day, taking or picking up personnel at the BIAP. We'd leave the Sadeer around 0700 with anyone there needing transport. Then we'd go to the Baghdad hotel to do the same; then we'd make a run to the BIAP, which took us through the "green zone." Again, we had to go through security checkpoints manned by our military.

There are several monuments of interest in the "green zone": Assassin's Gate, Hands of Victory, and Monument to the Unknown Soldier.

The BIAP was a huge complex which included the airport and several military camps or FOBs (Forward Operating Bases), and it was heavily fortified and secured. To get into the place wasn't too bad for us since we were DOD contractors with ID's, which we showed to the U.S. military on duty at the front entrance. We were also required to download our weapons before entering. Due to the security situation, you had to show your identification and were subject to search before you could enter a chow hall, px, etc. Iraqi civilians wanting access had to go through a little more; they were ID'd, their vehicle was searched, and there were K-9 handlers inspecting the vehicles for explosives. There was always a long line of cars trying to gain entrance. The really good thing about all this was being able to eat at an army chow hall which had much better chow than the Sadeer and a much larger selection. Being able to visit "Wal-Mart"; that was the nick name for the big PX. It was huge; it could have passed for a Wal-Mart. It had anything you needed and everything you didn't.

There was also a Burger King, Bazaar-type shops, coffee shops, PX car sales, etc. One of Saddam's palace compounds is also in the BIAP complex. I said we made runs everyday while I was assigned; the exception was several days before and after January 30, 2005, the day of election for the 275 member Iraqi National Assembly. We had to stand down due to security issues. An opening was posted for the movement control team, which I put in for. Of course I didn't get it; what was I thinking?

ASSIGNMENT: BASRA

On the sixth of February, I was assigned to the nether region of Iraq; "Jack" had exacted his revenge. I received an assignment to the Basra region, which is southeast of Baghdad, north of Kuwait, and west of the Iranian border. Several others were also assigned in the Basra Region along with me. Jonathan "Rabbit" Haynes, who was in the group that I came over with, was one. When we were in Kuwait, we had been asked who would volunteer to go to the Jordan Academy to instruct. I declined, but Rabbit was one that had accepted. Rabbit was a good old country boy from Mobile, Alabama and spent several years in the Navy in addition to being a cop. There were two others being transferred with us. One officer was from North Carolina, I believe, and was assigned as the Deputy Regional Commander in the Basra area. Now, in our conversation, he stated he was not going to sit behind his desk like so many others in mission. He promised to get out and see the "troops" and see what they actually do on the ground. We had to await military transport to Basra and did not leave Baghdad until the tenth. We flew on a C-130 to the Basra airport. Basra was under British control, and the airport had been a British airfield in the 30s and 40s. We had to fly on a helicopter from the Basra airport to the U.S. Embassy on February 11. It was pretty cold, and we spent several hours waiting on the flight line.

Basra was under British control during WWI and was turned over to the Iraqis in the 1930s. During WWII Basra's port, which is on the Shatt Al Arab River, was used to funnel supplies to the Soviets. Basra was also at one time a large tourist center and is Iraq's second largest city. The U.S.

Embassy compound in Basra was another one of Hussein's palace complexes, which is also located on the river. Hussein had numerous palaces all over Iraq, and I was told he would require his staff at each to prepare three meals every day in case he showed up; he moved around for security reasons. Too bad, if someone could have taken him out, it would probably have saved us a great deal of trouble.

In 1988, Hussein visited Basra after it was liberated from the Iranians. He was impressed with the area so decided he needed a palace on the Shatt. During construction, many homes were demolished to make room. Hussein also had a date palm plantation across the river leveled to prevent anyone with assassination plans from hiding there. The 1990 invasion of Kuwait slowed construction but did not halt it; even U.N. sanctions did not stop it. The locals didn't care for Hussein and vice versa. In 1991, an insurrection in the area was ruthlessly put down. The palace was completed and contained elaborate woodwork, Italian marble, and numerous sandstone carvings. Meanwhile, the locals were living in filth and poverty. It's my understanding Hussein never again came to the area after his initial visit. I and the other newcomers were able to tour some of the buildings, and even though they had been stripped and gutted, they were still quite impressive and must have been a sight to see in their day. The view of the Shatt from the Embassy was also pretty impressive.

U.S. EMBASSY

The embassy was not a large compound, and most of the security was handled by a company called Triple Canopy. Most of the security guards were from Central or South

America; for some reason Sandinista death squads came to mind. In all seriousness, they all seemed pretty professional. The perimeter of the Embassy was made up of eight to ten-foot-high concrete barricades, complete with guard towers. The river side of the complex was patrolled by the Brit military in small open boats. There were also a number of Americans working for Triple Canopy; their main function was to provide security for State Department personnel. The embassy was also home to (a base for) a Brit military contingent. There were numerous buildings on the compound. The living quarters were generally tin trailers similar to the Academy. However, these were better in that they only had two "bedrooms" to a unit and a shower and toilet used by one or two people, a welcome improvement. It also had the same kind of cheesy bed as the Academy, a fridge, desk, armoire, and internet connection when it worked. The Embassy got mortared or rocketed on occasion, and the trailers had a tin roof with no cover and a low single wall of HESCOs around them; not real safe in a serious attack. Fortunately Basra was a much quieter area than Baghdad. The chow hall was small, but the food was excellent. I guess all the State Department officials had something to do with that.

C.P.A.T.T.

The Basra C.P.A.T.T. (Civilian Police Assistance Training Team) office was staffed by some good people. The Regional Commander was from Philadelphia; he was a big, muscular, bald-headed guy. A tall, thin redhead from Chicago was the personnel clerk; a burly, laid-back officer was the operations chief; "Doc," who was a retired Navy Corpsman was the logistics guy; there was a "company" medic. Two guys there that I got to know fairly well were Scott Parker and Mark Preist. They were the SWAT and commando training officers and also the C.P.A.T.T. movement officers, responsible for the planning and execution of any travel done outside the Embassy compound. When we first arrived, none of us but the Deputy Commander had a job ready for him. It took several days before it was decided where we were needed and would be assigned. Scott and Mark were both professional and knowledgeable and were responsible for not only training the SWAT unit in the area, but they also conducted training for the I.P.L.O.s.

On the fifteenth, Scott and Mark put on an exhibition at the Embassy with the local SWAT team. It was observed by numerous Brit army and police officials. The training was conducted in an abandoned bank building which, like all the other buildings of the complex, had been stripped and looted. There were hundreds of Iraqi coins all over the ground; all you had to do was kick around a little sand, and you could collect handfuls as souvenirs. The team looked very professional and well trained. The goal was to train and equip teams in every area in the region.

On the seventeenth, several of us took a trip with Scott and Mark to conduct an inspection on one SWAT team and their facilities. Outside the main gate, along the Shatt, you could see the evidence that at one time it had been a major port and waterway; there were numerous rusting hulks that had once been seafaring vessels. Some were still afloat, some were sunken remains, and some were lying on their side in the mud of the river. Now, although Basra was not nearly as violent as Baghdad, the potential was there and travel was taken seriously just the same. While Mark and Scott took care of business, the soldiers occupied themselves by playing volleyball with some of the Iraqi SWAT members.

On the twentieth, we took a trip to the Shatt Al Arab Hotel, which housed another Brit army contingent. It was at one time a four-star hotel, and Basra was a well-visited tourist attraction. The Shatt Hotel also had a C.P.A.T.T. presence whose duties were to work with the local police stations. They were housed in the same kind of accommodations as the Embassy. The chow there was horrible, but it did have a small PX and Pizza Hut if you wanted a change of pace.

Most of my time was spent waiting around at the Embassy. It did have a decent gym which I frequented to occupy my time and try to maintain some semblance of shape. I mentioned Triple Canopy; some of the American guys were big boys. I'm not accusing anyone of anything, but on a couple of occasions, I did see empty steroid containers in the trash bin outside my sleeping quarters. There was also a DVD library in the gym. Both were run by a real nice Brit gentleman, what else at a Brit camp? He sold pins and patches he got from the "souvenir guy" at the Al Sadeer. I thought that was comical. Capitalism knows no bounds, I guess. The Embassy also had a bar called the "Screaming or Squealing Donkey" where you could get a beer if you wanted; it also had a little makeshift theatre that played movies several nights a week.

We finally got an assignment. Rabbit was assigned to Al Shaiba in the Basra area, and another officer named Larry Curtis and I were assigned to As Samawah, which is a town northwest of Basra, in the Al Muthana province. Larry had been at the Embassy, waiting to get another assignment in the region. It was decided Larry would accompany me to Samawah to assess the situation there. Larry was retired from a Wyoming Police Department. On the twenty-second, we convoyed Rabbit to Al Shaiba. It was a decent camp run by the Dutch. It had a decent PX and the typical tin can accommodations, except these actually had a metal roof designed to withstand indirect fire attacks.

AS SAMAWAH

Samawah was built on both banks of the Euphrates with hundreds of palm groves, which give it a tropical air and some relief from the oppressive desert heat. The city is predominantly Shia. At one time there was a population of Jews, but they were driven out in the 40s and 50s by Arab Nationalists. There is currently a small number of Assyrian Christians in Samawah. There is some industry in the area: a small oil refinery functions, a cement factory, and a railway overhaul facility. The railway facility was actually right across from the Brit camp in Samawah. We passed it on numerous occasions, and I never saw much activity there as opposed to the cement plant. There are some other things of interest in the area like Lake Sawa, a saltwater lake that is twenty-five miles north of Samawah and has no known source, and it was a tourist attraction in the past. A historical point of interest is the ruins of the ancient Sumerian city of Uruk, which dates back to 4000 b.c. The first written script was discovered there, dating back to about 3300 b.c. Again, Iraq is where ancient Mesopotamia, the cradle of civilization, once was.

CAMP SMITTY

On the sixth of March, Larry and I packed up our gear to leave the Embassy. It had been arranged for us to travel with a Triple Canopy convoy that was transporting some State

Department officials to Samawah for a meeting. Larry and I were issued an armored Suburban to drive to Samawah for our own use. A Marine captain rode along with us. He was a pleasant guy; in our conversation, he said he was involved in developing and maintaining a security plan for the oil pipelines in the region. I told him good luck with that because that had to be a daunting task. The trip took several hours, and the captain sacked out in the truck. I was driving, so that wasn't an option. Even if I wasn't, I couldn't envision myself ever being comfortable enough to sleep at anytime while traveling in that country. Larry and I were assigned to Camp Smitty outside Samawah, and when we arrived, it was run by the Dutch. Since it was the rainy season there, the place was an awful muddy mess.

The Dutch military didn't strike me as being a very professional organization. A lot of them looked sloppy and unsoldierly. Some were clean shaven; some weren't. Some of the female soldiers wore tongue rings. I saw at least one soldier sporting a pony tail; I thought he was a civilian worker. I was told later that the Dutch army had some kind of union or something. I was thinking of them in combat, voting on whether they would take a particular hill. That's just crazy. It's no wonder we have the greatest military in the world; it's still ruled by discipline. It's not surprising we take the lead in most military operations. We're one of the few powers in the free world, I guess, that has a military with any real pride, drive, or professionalism. The chow hall was a large tent with a dirty muddy floor, and the food was awful. Breakfast consisted of stale bread, cereal, and cheese. Lunch was more stale bread, sliced lunch meat type stuff, and cheese. I don't remember what dinner consisted of. I know I was probably spoiled, but I know what army chow can be, and I felt bad for these guys because their chow sucked. Even they would ask what it was they were being served. There was a small snack bar run by civilians on Smitty where you could get a sandwich or milk shake. Needless to say, they did a brisk business.

Their shower facilities were square metal containers, and the shower stalls were plastic "envelopes" you zipped up; it looked like you were showering in a Ziploc bag or something. We spent our first night in a freezing tent on a cot with no blankets; good thing we had a sleeping bag. It was apparent we hadn't been expected. The next day we were able to see the quarter master and get some sleeping quarters, another tin trailer.

The living areas were long rows of individual trailers on each side of a long metal grate walkway which was raised off the ground. The trailers were similar to the ones at the Embassy except the shower and toilet was in a separate container. There was a wall of sandbags around the rows of trailers but no overhead cover. Larry and I shared a trailer which had a bunk bed and a cot in the room which he chose to sleep on instead of the bunk bed. We had been issued a TV, DVD player, small fridge, and some office equipment at the Embassy. At least we could watch movies and have some cold drinks; the simple pleasures in life sometimes go a long way. Whoever had lived there before had fabricated some makeshift shelves with some boards and parachute-type cord secured to the ceiling with screws. Again, we had to go through somewhat of a hassle to get a trailer; this showed us no real plan was in place for our coming to Smitty.

Even though this was the Brit sector, the Dutch were running Smitty. After two or three weeks, more Brit units came, took over the camp, and the Dutch packed up and went home. Hallelujah! In time things began to improve dramatically. They cleaned up the mud and put down gravel and raised walkways and brought in more and better toilet and shower containers. Eventually a decent little PX and recreation center was built, which included a satellite TV, pool table, ping-pong tables, candy, and cold drinks. There was a pub built on camp, and it was open on Thursday night, and the soldiers were allowed to drink two beers, I believe. The perimeter of the camp was nothing more than sand/dirt bulldozed up into a wall about ten to twelve feet high. The wall was dotted with guard towers, and there was a zigzag of concrete barricades at the front gate to control vehicle traffic.

The chow hall (tent) was still a mess, and it took the Brits a while to clean it up. The tent had holes in it, and the A.C. didn't work half the time. When it warmed up, I remember sitting and trying to eat, drenched in sweat and fighting the flies for my food. The food quality greatly improved, although some of it took getting used to. They ate stewed tomatoes, really greasy fried eggs, fried bread—yes, fried bread—bangers (sausage), boiled bacon, and really awful watered-down juice for breakfast. They ate pork and beans three meals a day, too. Although, I really learned to like beans on my chips (French fries). They only served fish and chips a few times, which was a disappointment. Although the Brits weren't as well feed as American soldiers the food overall was good and the cooks did the very best they could with what they had.

ARMOR GROUP

When Larry and I arrived at Camp Smitty, we were the first and only American cops there. There was a group of British cops that worked for a company called Armor Group and had been there for several weeks and were just laying the groundwork to train the local Iraqi Police. Armor Group is basically the Brit version of the "company" I worked for, recruiting and training retired or former cops to go on overseas police missions.

"Edmond" was the Armor Group officer in charge when Larry and I arrived. And his unofficial second was "Danny." "Edmond" seemed to have a little attitude against Americans or American cops, and he never missed an opportunity to take a shot at me. At first I tried to hold my tongue and give him due respect. Eventually I got tired of it and fired right back at him. There were several other officers there, and all were great guys. I learned a little later that they weren't too fond of "Edmond" or "Danny" either. The Brit cop in overall charge of the program was a Chief Inspector from Northern Ireland with the R.U.C. (Royal Ulster Constabulary). He was nice enough; it just seemed sometimes he was a little overwhelmed by the task at hand and also the oppressive heat.

I worked more closely with three of the officers in particular: Paul Scarfe, David McNeillie, who were both from England, and Jon Brown, who was from Ireland. David was former British army, and Jon had worked in Belfast Northern Ireland. Jon shared a few stories with me about his experiences when the I.R.A. was still a serious threat. There were other officers from Scotland, Wales, and New Zealand, too.

Sometimes it was difficult to understand some of them with the accent and the vocabulary they used, such as knackered, kit, bangers, blokes, etc. It took me a while to catch on to some of it. I think the first time one of the Welsh officers was talking to me, I had no idea what he had said; I looked at Paul and David and asked, "What did he say?"

Paul, I believe, answered back, "I have no bloody idea!" I asked him if he was serious. He said that he was and that, "Sometimes I can't understand the Irish or Welsh blokes." I think my favorite expression was, "That's a good lad." There was one officer from Wales, and for some reason the other officers liked to harass him about his fondness of sheep. Actually they all ragged on each other about their family tree and where in the U.K. they hailed from.

OUT ON A LIMB

As I said, the Armor Group guys hadn't been there too long and were just getting started evaluating the status and needs of the police in the area. This was the Brits' show. Larry and I were sent to Samawah to work with no real direction and no real support. We were told to train and mentor but were given no specific goals or guidelines. Realistically, we were to "wing it." We were promised we would get everything needed to function: our own office trailer, living quarters, internet, toilet, and shower facilities. We were promised more officers, but nothing ever materialized. There were officers working back in Basra and out in other areas in the province, and from what I understand, they had many of the same problems we had but not nearly as bad. Larry and I ended up depending on the Brits out of necessity; we had one vehicle and only two of us, so we couldn't go anywhere on our own and could only travel with the military. Well, their assets were limited, and Armor Group had a leg up on us and had priority. We also had to share their office (tent) space and their internet connection. I always felt like a "ginger (red) headed step child."

AHMET

One thing we did have was an excellent interpreter. Ahmet was our interpreter. He was a tall, thin man in his thirties with glasses. He was intelligent and had studied veterinary medicine at one time. Armor group had a pool of several interpreters they used. Ahmet was exceptionally good; he clearly had a good understanding of the English language. Not only that, but he could at most times read between the lines of what and how we were asking something. This was very important and an ability most of the other interpreters lacked.

Some interpreters had a rudimentary understanding and couldn't grasp the subtlety, innuendo, or underlying meaning of some questions or answers. Ahmet was candid and did not try to mask the meaning of what we asked or how it was answered. Some L.A.s were afraid, I think, to ask certain questions. They were hesitant to ask blunt questions and tried to sugarcoat some answers directed at us. Armor Group tried to use him when he was available. Ahmet had an infant child that was ill; I never quite understood the exact problem. He was proud, and didn't talk much about it. Larry and I spoke to the doctors at the camp hospital for help. We were told they couldn't get involved. I'm not certain what happened to the baby.

THREE STOOGES

I ended up working with David and Paul. They were both great guys, and we resembled the three Musketeers or the Three Stooges or Three Amigos—not sure which. I learned as we went along Davie was fiercely patriotic. I think he was still upset about the outcome of the Revolutionary War, and he definitely disliked Mel Gibson. I can't repeat the "terms of endearment" he used to describe Mel. But he hated his movies, *The Patriot* and *Braveheart*. He considered them anti-British. David was also quite a history buff. The Brits talked about being Geordies, Cockneys, etc. I had no idea what all this was.

GEORDIES VS. COCKNEYS

David told me he was a "Geordie" from the north of England in the Newcastle area, and "Cockneys" were from London, and they hated each other. I thought I had issues with the whole Yankee and Rebel thing, being from the South. David went on to explain the term "Geordie" originated because they supported King George II when the "Jacobites," (Catholic Scots) led by Bonny Prince Charlie, invaded England in 1745. Prince Charlie was defeated, and England remained Protestant. Dave was also a Fusiliers soldier in the Brit Army in Northern Ireland in the 1980s. I was also surprised that neither Paul nor David was extremely fond of Princess Diana. I was under the impression all the Brit people were in love with her.

If I remember correctly, there were about eighteen police stations in the Samawah area, and we were tasked to go to about nine of them and conduct an assessment at each. The assessment was very basic: number of officers and policemen allotted, assigned, present, equipment allotted, assigned, and on hand. Equipment included weapons—pistols, AK-47s, machine guns, and ammunition. We were also to record vehicle information and office-type equipment, radios, etc. All the stations were in serious want of all types of equipment. Even so, I did observe that the I.P.s who were in charge of the arms rooms at the stations did take pride in the order and neatness they maintained. They also kept the weapons as clean as they could under the circumstances.

EVALUATING POLICE STATIONS

We were also to evaluate the training level of the stations. Now, the C.P.A. (Coalition Provisional Authority) had cleaned house with the military and police, but there were still I.Ps with twenty or thirty years experience. If a policeman was on duty prior to the invasion in 2003, they were required to complete a three-week course called T.I.P. (Transition Integration Program). It was designed to "de-Baathify" and indoctrinate the officers to democratic-style policing. I couldn't help but think three weeks was far too short to erase decades of police doctrine under a dictator. If they were hired after the invasion, they were required to attend a full eight-week academy. The goal was to retrain current officers and train new ones as rapidly as possible. There were some who were wearing a uniform with no training. Larry's team concentrated on meetings with the mayor and chief of police and other officials in Samawah.

STATIONS IN DISREPAIR

Now, most of the stations were very old and in serious disrepair—cracked and crumbling walls, plaster peeling off ceilings, broken windows, broken light fixtures, broken furniture, dirty and strewn with trash. These are the names of some of the stations we visited: Al Samawah Police Directorate, Al Samawah, Al Hurea, Al Najme, Al Warkaa, Al Hilal, Al Jamoury, Al Kazum, Al Muthana Police Directorate, and Al Majed. Just names difficult to pronounce, eventually to be forgotten, but each manned by men trying to protect and rebuild their communities with what little they had.

Some were in the immediate area of Samawah, and several were in the outlying areas. A few were up to two hours away. When we went to a station, we convoyed with the military in an Armor Group Toyota SUV, which was armored. I'm not sure how many, but some were Brit outposts from the 1930s; Al Hilal was one. Like I said, most of the stations were in serious condition, especially in the outlying areas. All were lacking to some degree or other—electricity, water, or working sanitary facilities. Most had little or no real security measures in place. Some stations had a little concertina wire strung out, or maybe a waist high concrete block wall, or maybe a three or four foot berm of dirt. There was nothing in place which would provide any real protection from an attack. It's a miracle that the area was generally quiet. It was really sad, and I couldn't believe the conditions these guys had to work in. I can't help but feel guilty thinking of things I have griped about as a cop. These cops knew what it was to work in a harsh environment and to do without. The Brit military worked on addressing the security issues, and I completed several reports to the Brit engineers myself. But this was Iraq, and apparently nothing happened quickly.

BRIT ARMY

Every time we went out, there was a military escort which was provided by either A or B Squadron of 1st The Queen's Dragoon Guards (The Welsh Cavalry). Our Suburban and the Armor Group vehicles had more protection than the vehicles they used, which were four-wheel drive Land Rovers. They had an open or closed back and had no armor to speak of and two soldiers would stand up in the rear as gunners with no real protection. We would travel in the middle of the convoy for our security. The Brits had "Warrior" armored vehicles, and about two months after arriving at Smitty, an Australian unit arrived with ASLAVs (Australian Light Armored Vehicle) and conducted patrols from Smitty.

I wasn't invited to any upper echelon or in depth intelligence briefings or operations planning but to me it seemed the Brits were pretty low-key in their day-to-day operations—nowhere near as aggressive or proactive as the American forces. They were very concerned about offending the local populace and, for example, were not supposed to wear their helmets because it seemed too aggressive. They were always told to "smile and wave." Maybe the area was generally quiet because of this attitude or because they were so passive and did not stir anything up. The soldiers on the ground just obeyed orders from the higher-ups. Whether this attitude was driven by military or political reasons, I don't know. The Brit army is like ours in that it is well trained and professional. Their soldiers complain like ours—and rightfully so. A soldier's life can be tough, and I can sympathize, having been one. Like our army, some of their officers are down-to-earth, and some are pretty pompous and arrogant. Before every scheduled station visit, the military squad we were assigned to go out with would have a mission briefing. This usually consisted of any relevant intelligence information, route to be taken, alternate route, action to be taken in case of emergency or hostile action, etc.

A contingent of the Japanese Self-Defense Forces worked in Samawah from January 2004 to 2006. They were there to perform humanitarian tasks and worked on building or repairing several water treatment and purification facilities. They were not allowed to do any combat operations; I think this dates back to the conditions set after WWII. Their camp was just down the road from Smitty. I never got an opportunity to visit the camp, which I was told was immaculate. On occasion the Japanese camp got hit by a rocket or mortar, or a patrol was hit by a roadside bomb. I guess the bad guys never heard the saying, "Don't bite the hand that feeds you." Some people just have no sense and are blinded by hatred; the Japanese were there to help the people and were not kicking down doors or conducting offensive operations such as that.

SPINNING OUR WHEELS

It took several weeks to visit all the stations and collect the data that was needed. Like I said before, we were getting no real guidance from Basra as far as mission goals, objectives, or any logistical support. We were required to send a daily report to the operations officer at the Embassy. This in itself was sometimes difficult; if the internet in the Armor Group tent was down or unavailable, I had to go to the military internet trailer. These were a real pain because first of all, you had to wait in line, and when it was 140 degrees outside, that wasn't fun, and most of the time, the AC didn't work, so it was hotter inside than out. When you finally got to a computer terminal, it was limited because you couldn't attach or download files. Not sure what happened to that information because as much as we reported the deficiencies, nothing happened. In all fairness, the Brits weren't able to get much in the way of equipment either.

After going to the same stations over and over and not really being able to do much of anything or improve their situation, I at times felt a little embarrassed. In Iraqi culture—Middle Eastern culture, for that matter—it is considered a sign of weakness to say "no" or "I don't know" or "I can't do that." I learned very quickly not to say no, but "I'll look into that" or "I'll see what I can do." I learned never to commit to anything one way or another. This was difficult for me. When we first started visiting the stations, we were treated politely, offered chai (hot tea), etc. But after a while, when the station commanders figured out we really couldn't offer them any real help, they treated us with skepticism. At that time, I didn't really feel like I was accomplishing much. This played on my mind because I, like most of the others I knew, had come to try and make a difference and accomplish something tangible.

RANGE DAY

On the eighteenth of March, Larry, Paul, Davie, Jon, some of the others, and I were invited to go to the shooting range with the military. Well, it really wasn't a range; we just went to a desolate area of the desert—okay, a *really* desolate area used by the soldiers before. There were some sheep and goat herders in the area, and that could have been a safety issue. The soldiers were qualifying with their personal weapons, the SA 80 and their LMGs (light machine guns), which are basically the equivalent of our Army's SAW (squad automatic weapon). They also broke out some AK'47s. I enjoy firearms of all types and have a small collection myself, so I never pass up an opportunity to shoot different weapons, especially fully automatic ones. The Armor Group guys carry a version of the Beretta assault rifle, an AR 70, I believe. We took turns shooting each others' guns. The Brits really seemed to like my M-4 carbine.

SWAT TEAM SELECTION

Around the end of March and the beginning of April, we received a directive from Basra to coordinate with the military and select a team to go to Baghdad for a four-week SWAT course. Larry Curtis was much more involved in this than I. Officers from Samawah TSU (Tactical Support Unit) were asked to come to the rail facility for testing. The TSU was a paramilitary Police unit consisting of around seven hundred men. The testing consisted of a PT test, team building tasks, and an obstacle course. The selection process was conducted at the rail facility across from Smitty. A forty-man team out of about one hundred prospective members was selected and transported to the BIAP (Baghdad International Airport) complex where special teams were being trained, including SWAT units.

APRIL LEAVE

I took leave from April 12 through the 27. As I said before, travel was complicated in Iraq. So far I had taken leave from Baghdad. It really got complicated the further from Baghdad you were. From Smitty, I had to ride a troop bus to Talil Air Base; this was a two-hour trip in an unarmored vehicle. A convoy ran several times a week to and from Talil to take and pick up Brit soldiers from leave. From Talil, I flew to Basra and stayed overnight at the Embassy. On the tenth, I flew to Baghdad and stayed two nights in the Sadeer.

Actually, I stayed in the "blue building"; this was another building in the same compound. The Sadeer was for officers permanently assigned and the "blue" was for transients. The "blue" was a real dump—that's all I can say. Glad I only had to stay a couple of nights. On the twelfth, I rode with the movement control team to the BIAP. This gave me a chance to visit and catch up. Can't remember if I saw my buddy "Jack." I wanted to tell him what a wonderful time I was having at Camp Smitty. From Baghdad, I flew to Amman Jordan, to Frankfurt, to Chicago, and finally to Jacksonville. A short respite back in civilization was always welcome— the key word is *short*. Nothing major was going on; I went to a wedding of some friends' daughter, just hung out, and relaxed with family. It was always in the back of my mind that I had to go back. I returned to Baghdad the twenty-ninth of April.

BABYSITTING

When I arrived, I was taken to Camp "X" where the SWAT guys were training. I met up with Larry who brought me up to speed on what was going on. The SWAT team had already completed several days of classroom instruction, firearms, and practical exercises. I don't have a SWAT background and neither did Larry; we were designated as "mentors" for the team. This really boiled down to being glorified babysitters. We were to observe, make sure the team got to chow, and class on time. We had no active part in the training. The instructors were contractors with an American company. I believe they all seemed to be pretty professional and experienced. I talked to one who was actually from the west side of Jacksonville, Florida. So we had some things in common, places, etc. One instructor was called "Boomer." None of the instructors went by their real names; we all had "handles." Mine was "Gator" and Larry was "Cheyenne." Boomer was an older man; he was very congenial, and in talking to him, I discovered he was quite experienced in combat, particularly special operations.

DISCIPLINE IS A GREAT THING FOR BOYS

We learned very quickly that not only our group, but most of them, were sorely lacking in discipline. There was an exception to this though. There was a group that consisted of Kurds that was very tough and well disciplined compared to most of the others. Most of the instructors were fairly laid-back in their treatment of the trainees; a couple of the younger ones were more gung-ho and verbally abusive. One incident occurred when some of the trainees had failed to do what was asked and were told to "schnau," or do push-ups. Well, they weren't too crazy about the push-ups, but they accused the instructor of cursing at them or insulting them in some other manner. I wasn't there, so I don't know what actually happened. It took some convincing to calm the trainees down and get them back into training mode.

GOT A CIGARETTE

When the team left Samawah, they were told to pack enough stuff for thirty days of training. I have to say, in this respect, I felt some sympathy for them. The living conditions were pretty sparse for them. They had a bunk and nothing else, no lockers or anything; they lived out of their suitcase or, in most cases, a plastic bag. There was also no laundry service, so they were washing their clothes in the bathroom sinks. Their shower facilities weren't that great, either. Well, they got to a point where they were running out of cigarettes and asked Larry and me to get them some. There was no PX right on the camp for them, and I wasn't going to spend my money to buy cigarettes. I didn't smoke, so I had little sympathy in this respect. Larry and I told them there wasn't much at this time we could do. Well, this almost turned into a mutiny. They were adamant that they needed cigarettes and weren't going to continue training until they got some. Again, we told them that we didn't have any, but we'd "see what we could do" or "look into that." These guys were literally ready to pack up what little they had and leave.

We gave pep talks and patriotic speeches to try to change their minds. I told them to think about the "big picture," that they're receiving the best training they could get, and to think about their honor and their families and communities. I told them to think how much more able they would be to protect and defend their homes, families, and communities and not to throw it away over some cigarettes. To be honest, I got irritated and told Larry that if they wanted to go home, maybe we should send them. We were able to get one of the language assistants to get them some cigarettes in Baghdad and got the thing worked out. They missed a day or two of training, and I'm surprised the powers that be allowed them to stay. But there was too much money invested to cut them loose.

So the team went back to training. Most of the training I was present for was practical stuff. They had several decent "shoot houses" at the facility. These were mock-up buildings where the trainees could do live fire exercises. This portion included practice entry of buildings, room clearance using flash bangs, and engaging targets with live fire. After the "mutiny," the team performed pretty well and worked hard. I was a little nervous during the live fire portion, and I am thankful no one got shot in the back. The "shoot houses" had no ceiling and walkways, so the instructors could watch from above. I remember standing topside, watching the team train and mortar rounds exploding in the distance. The team was also taught how to do bus assaults and high risk vehicle stops.

GRADUATION

The team graduated on May 12. As part of the gradation, General Petraeus came to the camp and observed the ceremony, the teams also put on demonstrations for the General. The Samawah team demonstrated their bus assault techniques. Overall they looked very good. Prior to leaving, the team was issued refurbished AK-47s ,thousands of rounds of ammunition, body armor and trauma plates, gas masks, pistol belts, holsters, battering rams and assault tools, radios, chargers and tactical shields—pretty much anything a typical SWAT team in the states would have. Maybe not quite as high-tech, but all the basic equipment needed to function.

We flew back to Smitty on CH-47 (Chinook) helicopters after loading up the gear. The flight took several hours, and we flew at a fairly low altitude. I was seated in the rear looking out the back ramp that was open for the tail gunner. After a while, I dozed off to be awoken by flares being dropped by the pilot. At first I thought we were being attacked. For a few seconds, I was a little startled and grabbing for my weapon.

We arrived in Smitty around 0200 and unloaded the equipment, which we put into a metal conex. The SWAT team was taken into Samawah by a Brit patrol.

BACK TO WORK

When I returned from leave, there were several issues that were going to arise and need addressing. Prior to leave, Larry, myself, and several of the other Brits had been going to the local Police Academy. Wouldn't quite compare it the one in Jordan or even Baghdad, but it was functioning and conducting some decent training. Chris Sparks, who was another Brit with Armor Group, was mainly working on this issue. Chris was a short, stocky bloke and was an avid boxer. I wouldn't want to have to tangle with him. He had worked at a training facility in Az Zubayr and had been working with Samawah's facility since before Larry and I arrived at Smitty. The commander at the Academy was a Colonel Fadhil, who Chris had been working directly with to get the Academy up and running again. As far as I know, it had been functioning before the invasion in 2003.

COLONEL FADHIL

Colonel Fadhil was always polite and offered chai and snacks every time we visited. I remember one of the first meetings I attended with Chris. He was trying to determine what priority equipment was needed at the Academy. Chris' primary mission was to get the Academy up to speed and had support from higher up to get most of what he needed. Chris asked the colonel what he needed. The colonel requested a

TV, DVD player, office furniture, etc.—not the response I expected. I would learn that the colonel and other officers in the police and military always expected things. It was a situation of "Okay, I'm going to let you come into my Academy and work, so what are you going to give me?" Not "Thank you for coming and training my policemen, but first what's in it for me?" It is part of the Arab culture that whenever you want to do something, you have to grease the big guy's palm, even though he's going to benefit from your actions.

Chris did an excellent job there, all things considered. Even though he was able to get necessary tools, none of the facilities I saw in Iraq would in any way compare to the U.S. He succeeded in conducting train the trainer, T.I.P., leadership, firearms, and other training courses. The Brit military was also involved in much of the training and, of course, provided security anytime we were at the Academy or at a police station. I was only involved in a limited capacity in the training; I was only involved with firearms. Again this was the Brits' area of responsibility and pretty much their show.

GROUPS FOR JORDAN

Larry and I received another directive from Basra. This time it was to prepare candidates for the Jordan Academy. This process started late in May and took several weeks. The process was similar to what we did at the Academy in Baghdad. With the absolutely necessary help of the Armor Group officers and L.A.s, we administered a literacy test and pt test and had the candidates complete a standard application, Baath party forms, etc. On June 26, we had a group of about sixty report, and on the twenty-fourth of July, another group of about equal size reported to the Academy. Once they were checked off our roster and loaded onto buses, they were escorted by the military to Talil Airbase and flown to Jordan.

SWAT TEAM ISSUES

From the time Larry and I returned with the SWAT team from Baghdad, we had to work on several issues. The first was to issue their equipment; we had no way to get it to them without assistance from the military. When we tried to coordinate with the military, we were told that there was a hold on issuance of equipment. Our argument was that it had already been issued in Baghdad, and we only needed transport. Apparently it was discovered that the Dutch had issued equipment, especially weapons, without any real accountability, and there were hundreds of weapons not accounted for. At that point, the Brit patrols were tasked to go to each station in the area and do a complete weapons inventory. Since we had developed a pretty good rapport with the military and obviously depended on them to accomplish whatever we needed to do, we were glad, if not obligated, to assist in sorting the mess out. Well, I can't say that it was ever completely resolved, but I guess the numbers over time became a little more manageable, if not acceptable.

INTEGRATING SWAT

After several weeks, we were finally allowed to deliver the equipment to the SWAT team. This delay was a disappointment because we had really hoped to get them operational as soon as possible, at least while their training was still fresh in their heads. Another issue we had to address was to integrate them with the local police; this was easier said than done. The team had received basic but high-quality training and was obviously much better trained than the average I.P. But for some reason, the local police officials seemed skeptical as to what function they might serve, even after a demonstration of their abilities on May 19 at the Academy. A ceremony and demonstration was put on for the local military and police officials to showcase the Academy. It included the SWAT team, local riot control unit, TSU, and cadets from the Academy. All the participants looked pretty good overall. There was one I.P. who was an instructor putting on a martial arts demonstration. He was engaging in mock fights, showing off his prowess, kicking or karate chopping through concrete or plaster slabs, which had "terrorists" or "terrorism" in Arabic in black paint. He had some skill, but it was just humorous, and we nicknamed him "karate man."

TSU CAMP

On the eighteenth of June, I was selected to go to the TSU camp with the Bobbie in charge of the Brit police mission. Mr. Graham had a meeting with the TSU commander to address some issues. He was a nice man and seemed to be very professional, but he generally seemed to be high-strung and somewhat stressed out. I'm not sure how I was the lucky one to be chosen. There was a group at Smitty called CRG (Control Risk Group); this was a Brit company that was the U.S. equivalent of Blackwater or Triple Canopy, and they were transporting us to the meeting.

Well, it started out real well because as we were getting ready to leave the camp, I locked and loaded my weapons as usual. When I got into the vehicle, the team leader asked me what condition my weapons were in. I told him they were locked and loaded as they are whenever I leave camp. Well, we argued for several minutes about this. His angle was I was considered a "principal" or the person being protected and was not authorized to carry loaded weapons. I told the guy I was former military and police and knew how to handle weapons. I also informed him I worked for the U.S. State Department and was authorized to carry my weapons loaded. Well, this guy was a piece of work and didn't want to hear it. I finally figured I wasn't going to change this guy's mind, so I let it go and unloaded my weapons. Some people are like billy goats ramming their heads against a wall; this guy was one of them. Good news travels fast. When I got back to camp, the Armor Group guys were busting my chops, "Bloody yank can't go anywhere without making somebody mad."

We arrived at the camp with no problems; it was only about fifteen minutes away. The police stations in the area were bad, but I have to admit the TSU camp was really bad. It was nothing more than a dirt berm with concertina wire around it. There were two or three buildings made of concrete block. The rest were tin trailer-type structures. They had no real water source or sanitary facilities, and their only source of electricity was a generator, and this hinged on availability of fuel.

Two issues that were being discussed were the possible disbanding of the TSU and building a new camp for them. The debate at the upper levels was whether to outright disband the unit or roll it into the military or police force. Now, if they were disbanded, that led to the possibility of several hundred angry, jobless men with guns, which you didn't want. If they were rolled into the police, that meant they had to be trained adequately, which was another issue in itself. The other issue, which I didn't quite understand, was the construction of a new camp. If they were going to be disbanded, what's the need for a new camp? Apparently the Brit military was going or, at least at this point, planning to assist in its construction. I'm not sure how these issues turned out. One main objective we all shared was to get the police, TSU, and military to cooperate and supplement each others efforts.

PROMISED JOBS

Another situation arose in relation to jobs and local young men not having anything to do. Reportedly, at some time in the past, the Governor of Al Muthana province had promised a group of young men who were present at a protest jobs as policemen in the area. Well, apparently he tried to backtrack somewhat, and it caused more protests. He ended up apparently reiterating the promise to several hundred. This would have to be approved by the MOI in Baghdad, which I'm not sure if it ever was, but the governor gave it his blessing, and hundreds showed up at the Academy. This caused security issues, and riots nearly broke out. But for several days, the Academy staff processed these men in. We were not allowed to take part in this since it was not approved by the MOI, so in turn it was not sanctioned by our superiors.

DOG DAYS OF SUMMER

Smitty was out in the desert, obviously, so there were absolutely no trees on the camp, and during the dog days of summer, temperatures reached 130 to 140 degrees or higher. Severe dust storms were frequent also—not quite on the scale of *The Mummy*, but close. At the height of summer, the generators frequently overheated and shut down, turning our trailers, the chow tent, and the gym into saunas. But no matter how hot it got, the Brits loved their tea time. They were drinking tea, and I was dying for a cold drink of Gatorade. I guess things weren't hot enough for the soldiers; in June there were a couple of female visitors. They were adult magazine or film stars, and I can tell you they weren't wearing traditional female Arab garb. This whole thing just struck me as bizarre. They flew these two girls out into the middle of nowhere in stifling heat to "cheer up" the boys for a few hours. I'm all for the morale of the troops but can't help but wonder if it made the situation better or worse.

LAST SWAT MEETING

The last time I saw the Samawah SWAT team was July 27. We had delivered their gear, and we had been able to secure them a base of operations in the Intelligence Unit building. Their situation there was primitive but functional. But this made sense because they could work side by side with the intelligence officers and cooperate to develop any operational plans. They had, in fact, at this point, done several successful operations. Unfortunately Larry and I had not been able to observe any because trying to coordinate the availability of a military escort with the operations just didn't coincide. Another good point of this was they were somewhat independent, so this gave them control over their equipment and weapons. Larry, the SWAT guys, and I feared that some station commander or other higher up police official would get his paws on their gear for his own personal use or motives.

FATE OF SWAT

The idea which had been initiated in Basra was to develop a traveling SWAT mentoring team to travel throughout the region, checking on and training the different units. I don't know and doubt if this ever came to fruition. I really hate to think that all the money, training, gear, and potential as a police asset had gone to waste. But I really believe that's what happened. I know they were motivated to do a job, but it would be very easy for them to be disbanded, and their equipment disappear, especially without the oversight of Brit or American police or military.

END OF MISSION

I ended my assignment and left for home the second of August. By this time, I was tired, disillusioned, and very disappointed with my mission. I know you make the best of any situation—maybe there was more I could have done different to make it better—but there has to be direction and proper support. I hope that I had made a small difference somewhere along the way. I don't feel I didn't do a good job. I firmly believe I did the best I could with what I had.

It was difficult saying good-bye. I had worked with some good people. Larry and I had become pretty good friends. When you live in an eight by twelve tin can for months together, you either become friends or enemies. We had done the former. I don't know how many times we sat in the room at night watching *Blazing Saddles*, talking, or goofing around. I think we had every line of that movie memorized and never missed an opportunity to throw a line from it into the conversation to get a laugh.

When I left Smitty, I went through Basra to the Sadeer to out-process, inventory, and turn in gear. I can't remember if I saw the movement team leader, but I learned after I got home that he was severely wounded by a roadside bomb in September. I also learned from Larry that Colonel Fadhil from the Samawah Academy was assassinated.

STATUS OF SAMAWAH

The British military turned over the security to Iraqi forces and pulled out of Samawah in 2006. In December, elements of the Madhi Militia clashed with police in an attempt to take control of Samawah. All this news made me wonder if any of us had done or were doing any good.

HOMECOMING

It was great to be home. It takes quite a while to unwind and get back into reality, at least the reality of life back home. I took several weeks off to take it easy and spend time with my wife and family. My wife and I went on some weekend trips and spent a week in Lake Tahoe, Nevada. Life in America is good.

Lying around and taking it easy is nice, but after a while, it gets a little boring. I was anxious to get back to work and hoped to get rehired by the agency I had worked for before I went to Kosovo. I had approximately twelve years with the state of Florida and wanted to complete eight more for retirement. I stayed in contact with several friends who still worked there. I had also stayed in contact with the personnel manager and had completed an application months before. When I left in November of '03, the sheriff at that time told me I had a job when I returned. Well, that sheriff had been voted out and a new one in. I went through part of the hiring process, polygraph, and oral interview.

I had an interview, and I thought I had done very well and was told I would hear back in a week or two. Well, after several weeks, I got no word, so I called the personnel manager to see what was up. She told me she didn't know what was going on and would check on my file. Well, several more weeks went by, and I was finally told I would not be rehired.

Now, as I said, I was in contact with guys who were still deputies. I was told about deputies who were hired and had quit after a few weeks or months later. I heard through the grapevine later that the person that interviewed me thought I was too arrogant and acted like he owed me a job. All I can say is that's totally untrue, and I have no idea how he came to that conclusion. I made a point of being gracious and expressing my desire to be rehired, but unfortunately he did not see it that way.

FCCJ

I still needed a job and started looking elsewhere. It occurred to me that Tim Winterhalter told me in Kosovo he had a connection in Jacksonville that might help me out if I needed a job. I followed this lead and ended up as an adjunct instructor for FCCJ (Florida Community College at Jacksonville). The college had a naval contract teaching armed security courses to the sailors from local bases. It consisted of basic marksmanship, unarmed self-defense, use of pepper spray, and other security related classes. It was enjoyable, good experience, and something to put on my résumé. Unfortunately it was part-time, there were no benefits, there was little chance of moving up, and it wasn't really cutting it.

WHAT NOW

Well, after being turned down by my first choice and at this time unable to land something more than a part-time gig, I decided to reapply with the "company." Since I had prior mission experience, my application was "expedited." I still had to complete the same amount, physical exam, etc; it just meant my application was a little closer to the top of the stack. I was actually starting to miss overseas police work. Not so much Iraq but the people I had met and worked with. I actually requested Afghanistan; wanted to go to a different area but was told that there were no openings there with my qualifications, but there were plenty in Iraq. Right, well, I volunteered again. When would I ever learn? I guess I just missed the work, the challenge. I will admit I missed the pay, too. I was only making one or two grand a month as opposed to several times that overseas. I admit it gets addictive bringing in those big paychecks. I guess I had it in my blood now. I was told after a couple of missions it was difficult to return to "regular" police work.

SECOND IRAQ TOUR

TRAINING IN VIRGINIA AGAIN

Prior to every mission, police advisors are required by the State Department to complete a training and selection process. This is regardless of how many missions a person has completed. This session was from March 7 to 17, 2006, in Fredericksburg, Virginia. It was similar to the session I completed prior to Kosovo. The firearms' training was more intense—more range time with more emphasis on close quarters battle type shooting. We got a good deal of trigger time with AK-47s, too. The first aid was more geared to traumatic injuries or wounds. We also did convoy operations, reacting to ambushes and evacuating wounded persons from disabled vehicles, etc. This training also incorporated simunitions; this is similar to paintball rounds and adds some realism and fun to the training.

The training was much more intense and realistic. It definitely had a more serious air to it, and rightfully so. Things in Iraq were getting more deadly by the day, kidnappings, assassinations, roadside bombs, and sectarian violence. We also had more culture, map reading, health and nutrition classes, and intelligence and State Department briefings. We were also issued clothing and other equipment. Although I had been in the military, I had not seen actual combat, and no training can completely prepare one for that, and our training didn't really prepare me for the things I would see this tour.

INTERESTING CHARACTERS

The class was made up of around one hundred prospective officers. Most were, of course strangers, but there were two I knew: Mel Lankford from Kosovo and Scott Parker from my first Iraq adventure. We stayed at the Holiday Inn, and Scott and I roomed together. After Scott left Iraq, he had done a tour with Blackwater. He was a former police SWAT officer and paramedic. There were several others I got to know and hung out with during training: Mike Alberts from San Diego, Rick Roberti from New Jersey and Chad Hermes from Illinois. Mike was a good guy, "tatted" to the max, and a little high-strung. In fact, part of his e-mail address included "Tackleberry" at one time. Rick sounded like an extra from *The Sopranos,* and Chad was an easygoing muscle guy.

One officer in the class was in his seventies and wore a West Point ring. I spoke to him a few times; he graduated from the Military Academy before I was even born. If I remember correctly, he said Westmoreland was either an instructor or guest speaker who actually handed him his ring. He was a tough old guy and did as well as any of us. Unfortunately towards the end of training, he developed pneumonia and couldn't deploy. There's always one poor guy in the group whose name you can't pronounce or it gets made fun of. Well, our class had one and we all called him "Mr. Stick."

FT. BLISS

We were flown to Ft. Bliss on the eighteenth and remained there until the twenty-fourth. This was fundamentally the same as my initial Iraq tour. We had briefings, equipment and ID, cards issued, medical, dental exams and everyone's favorite: shots. I have learned one thing; hang on to your shot records because the Army will give an unlimited number of inoculations. No matter how much you protest you've had this or that shot, they don't want to hear it. If you can't prove it, you're getting it. Even some of the biggest, toughest guys will get weak-kneed after half a dozen shots or more. I lucked out and didn't need any fortunately.

We were given the option of staying at a local hotel instead of the army barracks if we wished to pay for it. I took advantage and spent a few more days with the wife. Bren had to leave the twenty-first, and I moved into the barracks. I roomed with Scott, Mike, Chad, and Rick. It was never a dull moment in that room.

KUWAIT

We left Bliss on the twenty-fourth and arrived in Kuwait on the twenty-sixth. Our flight to Kuwait included a stop in Bangor, Maine. It's well known for its patriotism and greeting our troops coming through the airport. They treated us very well, greeting us and shaking our hands. There's a room that has pictures of G.I.'s patriotic tattoos; Mike Alberts is now on the wall of honor there. While in Kuwait, we stayed in a Holiday Inn and didn't really do much waiting for transport to Iraq. It was another rollercoaster C-130 ride into Baghdad.

HOME SWEET BAGHDAD

We arrived at the BIAP (Baghdad International Airport) between noon and 1:00 p.m. on March 30. We waited until after midnight for a ride from there to our next destination.

We rode on a "Rhino," which is a military bus on steroids. It resembled an armored Greyhound; "Leave the driving to us." From the airport, we went to the "Green Zone" or "International Zone" where we stayed overnight in a freezing tent. March in Baghdad is cold. We were taken to the Al Sadeer hotel by the "Shark team." This was a convoy made up of former South African military and police. We were told we could not carry our weapons while in their vehicles. Believe me, we tried to argue the stupidity of that, but our efforts were futile. Been there, done that (Camp Smitty CRG team June 18, 2005). Well, I can tell you we all felt naked with no weapons in hand, and I prayed nothing would happen.

AL SADEER

I couldn't understand why the Sadeer and Baghdad were still being used; the bad guys had tried twice to blow the Sadeer up with limited success. Given that this was my second trip to Baghdad, I wasn't as impacted by the surroundings as most of the others. Scott and I roomed together again. My buddy "Jack" had long ago been fired, and there was a new personnel chief, a former officer from Texas. He was a decent guy; the only issue I had was he made the statement, "I'm allergic to going outside the wire." Now, once you hit the ground in Iraq, the danger level goes up for everyone, but I couldn't quite understand that statement.

BRIEFINGS

We had to endure the usual briefings and lectures regurgitated to every new group. On the fifth of April, Major General Joseph Peterson spoke and welcomed us to the mission. General Peterson was the military head honcho of the Police Mission. He welcomed us all and told us how important and appreciated we were. He told us 2006 was "the year of the police." On the seventh, a colonel from the 49th Military Police Brigade presented a class. The 49th was at that time responsible for the actual implementation of the Police Mission. C.P.A.T.T. (Civilian Police Assistance Training Team) worked in conjunction to accomplish the mission of training, mentoring, and inspecting the police to help bring them up to the standards set by the military.

REQUIRED REPORTS

We were briefed on the current objectives and reporting procedures. I freely admit I'm not the sharpest tool in the shed, and I can tell you some of this stuff was a bit confusing—to me anyway. All sorts of unfamiliar terms were thrown at us: PSMR (Police Station Monthly Report), DSR (Daily Station Report), Station Transition Readiness Assessment, and Station Assessment Checklists. The DSR was simple enough and was to be completed after every station visit and included information such as how many police were on duty, detainees, if training was conducted, and if the station had power during the visit.

DOES ANYBODY UNDERSTAND THIS STUFF

The really complex forms were the PSMR Station Assessment Checklist. The checklist consisted of about eight hundred questions ranging from personnel and finance issues to security and force protection and everything in between. Every question on the list was "weighted" as to its importance.

There were one hundred thirty that were considered most important, and they were labeled high, medium, and low. High on the list were areas such as being able to identify and arrest a suspect. Medium covered vehicles and communication equipment, and lower on the list were electricity, water, and sanitation.

The PSMR was to be completed monthly and was a compilation of the daily reports and the checklist. The PSMR was supposed to reflect a TRA Level (Transition Readiness Assessment) of 1, 2, 3, or 4. 1 meaning the station was 85% capable, 2 was 70% capable with support, 3 was 50% partially capable, and 4 was less than 50% and incapable. This was to be determined by a mathematical formula that I still don't comprehend. We as I.P.L.O.s (International Police Liaison Officer) were to work with our military team leader to accomplish this. We were also required to help formulate a ninety-day training plan based on the station's deficiencies.

REALITY AS I SAW IT

As I became more familiar to this, I realized to sincerely accomplish this, we would have to spend eight hours a day, seven days a week at the stations. Trying to do any meaningful training would also prove to be a disheartening task. The military was so over tasked, so actual station visits and time on station made it exceedingly difficult to pull off any consequential instruction. Furthermore, some of the goals such as computers for the stations seemed a little "cart before the horse" to me since most of the stations had little power, water, or sanitation facilities. Another issue, which was a hindrance more times than not, was only having one interpreter available on a station visit. The military usually had priority, and you had to wait for them to finish any tasks they had; then you could get the L.A. (language assistant) and complete yours.

ASSIGNMENT TIME

When the occasion came to choose an assignment, Scott Parker and I attempted to go to Basra. There was an operations chief slot available that we both attempted to put in for. We were informed it was only open to officers already in mission. Our dispute was we were both prior mission and had worked in and were familiar with Basra. Our arguments got flamed speedily. On the eighth, we were informed our assignment was Camp Rustamiyah. It was a former Iraqi Officer Instruction facility in the southeast of Baghdad. It was called Ar Rustamiyah College and was known as the "West Point" of Iraq. On the ninth, a group of our classmates left for Najaf where their assignments were.

CAMP RUSTAMIYAH

We moved to Rusty, Camp Rustamiyah, on the night of the eleventh in a convoy of Suburbans driven by officers assigned there along with a military escort. Scott, Chad, Mel, Mike, around twenty others, and I made the trip. The trip took some thirty minutes and was uneventful other than being crammed in the trucks like sardines. We unloaded our gear and then were shown our barracks. Scott and I ended up in a building housing soldiers away from our main barracks. Like I said, it was night so there's nothing like stumbling around in the dark in an unfamiliar place dragging three duffle bags of gear and a weapon trying to find your quarters.

GRAND TOUR

Rusty was renamed in September of 2004; it had been named Camp Cuervo in honor of PFC Ray Cuervo. PFC Cuervo was assigned to Apache Troop, 1st Squadron, 2nd Armored Cavalry Regiment and was killed in combat on December 28, 2003, in Baghdad. The camp was comprised of numerous two-story metal or concrete block and plaster buildings. The camp was decades old, so most of the buildings were pretty run-down but livable.

Our room actually had some old, dirty carpet on the floor, and the walls were painted dark brown. There were several black metal army bunk beds and metal wall lockers. The room and everything in it was painted varying shades of brown except the beds. We scrounged up a TV and fridge and bought a DVD player to make it a little homier. It was the season, and it rained just enough to turn the ground into mud. This was no ordinary mud; it was thick and stuck like glue and hardened like concrete. Rusty was not too bad overall; it had a well-stocked PX, three gyms, two chapels, laundry, hospital, several souvenir shops run by locals, and the chow hall was exceptional. There was also a detention facility; it was no secret, I guess, although you never heard about any of the goings-on there—not that low men on the totem pole such as me needed to know. It was a small concrete building surrounded by concertina wire. Any detainees brought in were transferred to Abu Ghraib after they were interrogated, I assume.

TRAINEE STATUS

The officer I was teamed up with had been at Rusty for several months and had been working with a military squad and already knew the "ropes." On the fourteenth, which was Good Friday, Scott and I went to IED (Improvised Explosive Device) training. It entailed reacting to different scenarios such as IED strike with wounded, disabled vehicle, etc. Beforehand, I had heard a rumor about an IPLO who had been involved in an IED attack and apparently didn't react very well. I never even heard the guy's name and can't judge. No one knows how they will act until it happens to them. All you can do is train and hope it kicks in under a stressful situation. On the twenty-eighth, we completed a CLS (Combat Lifesaver) course. This was an advanced first aid class, including how to start I.V.s. I took the course when I was in the army, and it's normally forty hours; we got the eight-hour condensed version.

We were told many times to integrate with whatever team we were assigned to. I tried to work hard and be as much a part of the team as possible; being former military helped a lot. I could relate quite a bit with the enlisted soldiers and their plight since I had been one once upon a time. Things had changed drastically since then, so I asked lots of questions to try and catch up. Even though we were generally treated well, there was on occasion a barrier separating us from the military. We were paid quite a bit more, and some had issues with that. Some felt we had no business being there at all. Most were young enough to be my sons or daughters, and I couldn't help looking at them in that respect from time to time. But I can say they were all extremely hardworking, dedicated, and patriotic. I know it sounds cliché, but they were truly America's best.

MISSION ANXIETY

My first go-round had been generally quiet and sheltered. This was the real deal; the roadside bombs, snipers, and ambushes were out there and could strike at any time. The insurgents did not differentiate between U.S. military and contractors; they had prices on all our heads. If you didn't get killed outright, you could end up hog-tied on the floor with some guy in black pajamas hewing your head off with a dull rusty knife, your blood gurgling in your throat as you tried to scream in pain. You had to decide what you would do in that situation: fight to the end or save the last round for yourself. I'm a Christian, but on the issue of suicide, I haven't come to grips one way or another and mulled over this quite a bit as I'm sure most others did, too. I've never had a terminal ill-ness or faced any other circumstance similar to that. I prayed I would have the courage not to be taken alive. Mostly I prayed not to have to make that choice.

FIRST TIME OUT

I'll admit I was anxious the first and last time I went out on a mission. For me it never wholly subsided. Every pile of dirt or trash and any parked car could be obscuring a bomb from sight. That tension was continually on my mind. Over the next two weeks, I went on four missions with my training officer. My first was on Easter Sunday, April 16. The chow hall put on a very nice dinner with all the decorations and fixings.

Each mission started with a briefing at least one to two hours—route to be taken, number of vehicles, passenger assignments, call signs, radio frequencies, stations to be visited, and objectives on station. Each Humvee crew had a primary and alternate assignment such as designated aid and litter, LZ (landing zone) marker, or recovery vehicle. Some of the jargon was Greek until I learned the route names, call signs, station names, etc. For the soldiers, it started much earlier; they had to perform vehicle maintenance, do communication checks to ensure the radio sets were operational, and check the GPS or navigational system. They had to mount weapons and load ammunition and other gear.

After briefing, you got into your designated Humvee, proceeded to a clearing barrel, which was a barrel filled with sand or sand bags, and you loaded your weapons. You left the camp at a prescribed time and navigated a circuitous route to the first station. The teams I rode with always tried to stay off the main routes as much as possible to avoid ambush or IEDs. This meant taking side roads, making unexpected turns, and sometimes doubling back—anything not to set a pattern or be predictable, which could make you a target. Every convoy I went out in contained at least four trucks.

ON STATION

Sadr city was horrible for the most part: garbage everywhere, dusty, some streets were completely flooded with sewage water, and in areas it was foul enough to make you gag. It broke my heart to see kids walking barefoot through the trash and other waste littering the streets. Once on station, soldiers designated as security would dismount and deploy to their assigned place to check the station and maintain an over watch. The driver and machine gunner always stayed in the Humvee. This was in case we needed to leave the station quickly and the gunners maintained security and would provide firepower if the station was attacked. You had to adopt an attitude of extreme vigilance at all times and to trust no one completely. Our lives literally depended on it.

You would meet with the station commander or the highest ranking officer present, and the first order of business was to obtain the information needed for your DSR (Daily Station Report), number on duty, etc. Then you would inquire about any significant activity or problems at the station recently. When time permitted, if you had cooperation, you conducted some type of police-related training. By and large a joint patrol with the I.P.s (Iraqi Police) was factored in to each visit. This consisted of driving in the area with one or more I.P. patrol vehicles intermingled in our convoy. Once the visit was complete, you went to the next station or returned to camp. Upon return to camp, you unloaded your weapons, the team leader would debrief if necessary, and the soldiers had to offload equipment and perform more maintenance.

258ᵀᴴ MP

On the thirtieth, Parker and I finally received a permanent assignment with the 258ᵗʰ MP Company, 3ʳᵈ platoon, 1ˢᵗ squad. Our team leader was a Staff Sergeant; his nickname was "Beef"—great guy, mid twenties, professional soldier, and—oh yeah—he was pretty big, too. Scott and I got along with all his soldiers and enjoyed working with them. They all treated us with courtesy and respect. Our squad was assigned to several stations in Sadr City, Al Nasir, Habibya, and Al Thawra traffic station. Scott and I had been assigned to a different officer on our first few station visits, and I can say I only had a very rough idea on what was going on, how things worked, what was expected, and what to expect.

Al Thawra station wasn't what I anticipated in regards to being a traffic enforcement unit. The officers were assigned at traffic intersections and simply directed traffic. However, they were well equipped and functioned quite well in their assigned duties. I never did figure out how they were so well supplied when the other stations were so lacking. During this time, police stations were being attacked regularly, but as far as I know, attacks on the traffic police were few or nonexistent. Guess they didn't pose any threat to the militia or insurgents. Al Nasir and Habibya were typical police stations. All were lacking adequate electricity; if the station had a generator, it was either broken or getting fuel to run them was an ordeal. All lacked a constant water supply, which in kind affected the toilet facilities. Toilets were not much more than a hole in the floor, and they don't use toilet paper. Believe me, they were bad. Some were literally enough to make you lose your lunch. All three were inadequate as far as facility security, insufficient walls, barricades, etc.

MAHDI INFLUENCE

Sadr City was under Madhi Militia influence, which was run by Muqtadr Al Sadr, and this didn't stop at the gates to the police stations. Outright, good old-fashioned corruption was in full swing, too. It took us several visits to meet the station commanders and senior officers and build up a rapport. We were tolerated more than anything, I think. Some of the I.P.s gave us "looks" and treated us with reservation. In all fairness, after time I learned many of the I.P.s desired to do the right thing but were outnumbered and hesitant to go against the militia for obvious reasons. I guess you were either part of the militia or you kept a low profile when it concerned them. We could come and do our business and go back to the camp; they and their families had to live there.

FRIEND AT HABIBYA

Habibya had one I.P. in particular that spoke very good English, and we developed a good relationship with him. He seemed to be genuinely forthcoming with us. He stated he was neither Sunni nor Shiite and did not care to be involved in the sectarian issues. He wanted peace for his country and to see a professional police force that was not swayed by religious or political winds. He told us he didn't mean any disrespect but didn't have much faith in the U.S. military. I asked why, and he said he had tried in the past to give intelligence information, but no one seemed interested or took him seriously. The Squad Leader passed his information up the chain of command to intelligence. To my knowledge, no one ever attempted to see if the guy had anything of value to offer.

OFF DUTY

Off duty time was spent in the same ways as in my other tours: working out, reading, watching movies, emailing, webcamming, and so on. Scott was a big outdoorsy guy, and he started us on volleyball, which occupied us as long as we could get enough for two teams or if it was interrupted by rocket or mortar fire. It was nice outside although temperatures were already reaching over a hundred degrees in May. We had fourteen missions in May for station visits, so I had a lot of downtime—too much gives you time to think about home and family though. Now, the soldiers didn't; they had maintenance, inspections, guard duty, other missions outside camp, etc. They got very little time off, which they needed and deserved.

MAY 8

May 8 was the first of many like experiences. Habibya was the station we visited that day. When we arrived, the I.P.s had recovered four bodies from an area about a mile northwest from the station. I had been around dead bodies as a cop with suicides, gunshot, hanging, stabbings, and car crashes, etc. but the things I saw this go round were an education for me.

The victims were all males in their twenties or thirties; they were bound, blindfolded, and shot in the back of the head at close range. A report had been written, lacking in detail and about a paragraph long. I've written longer reports on vandalism to a mailbox. Scott and I looked at each other in agreement; these guys had a long way to go.

TO THE CRIME SCENE

Parker and I told our Squad Leader that if it was cool, we wanted to go to the scene and try to do some crime scene work if possible. He always cooperated as much as he could and had to get the okay from his HQ first. One of the senior officers took us to the scene where we discovered four distinct pools of coagulated blood on the pavement and on the raised curb. I'm not a CSI expert, but it appeared all four had been made to kneel with their heads on the curb and were dispatched with one shot to the head. We found several spent nine millimeter shell casings around or mixed in with the blood. It did not appear any evidence collection had taken place.

BASIC CRIME SCENE STUFF

We gave a basic class to the Lt. Colonel and other I.P.s that had accompanied us; he was the station's lead investigator. We spoke about crime scene preservation, securing the scene, and basic collection of evidence. Possibly most importantly, we talked about doing a neighborhood canvass. Our answer was that the citizens wouldn't talk. This was true because they didn't trust the police and had no way of knowing if they might be talking to a militiaman or what. We stressed, however, that if the police were to be successful, this barrier would have to be overcome.

In all fairness, they had no system set up at that time to do any serious collection or evidence processing. I.P.L.O.s assigned with the major crimes units were trying to work on this issue, crime labs, crime scene vans, and evidence technicians were reportedly in the works. But at the local level, they had no way to collect, photograph, log, process or store it. I at first thought maybe this was due to the war, but after talking to other officers, it didn't seem there was any real system in place before that. At least that was my take on the situation. Under Saddam, you didn't need any evidence. After our mission, we felt we had actually tried to accomplish something but had a long road ahead.

LOST A COMRADE

Unfortunately our sense of accomplishment didn't last long. When we returned to camp, we learned a team from Charlie Company 1–147 Field Artillery 519th MP Battalion had been hit by a roadside bomb. An I.P.L.O. and a soldier had lost their lives in the blast. I didn't know the Sergeant, but he was a human being, a creation of God, a son, and a brother. I did know the I.P.L.O. because he had been in my training class. I didn't know him well, but we spoke on several occasions; he was always nice and seemed quiet. He was a Vietnam vet, a policeman of many years' experience, a husband, and a grandfather.

MEMORIAL

A memorial service was held at Rusty on the thirteenth, which included a roll call, taps, and a twenty-one gun salute. It was very emotional, and I know it was all I could do to keep my composure, but there wasn't a dry eye in the chapel. A really disappointing part of all this was that no one from C.P.A.T.T. showed up. I don't know why; I heard several rumors. The soldiers killed and wounded don't get enough airtime on the six o'clock news. The American public is probably even less aware of the number of police advisors and other contractors who have died there. May 8 had been a first—first of many victims of sectarian violence I would see and the first of many I.P.L.O.'S and soldiers from the camp that would give their lives in service of their country, for Iraq, and hopefully for a better world someday.

LAMBS TO THE WOLVES

Many of the units were National Guard or Reserves serving in Iraq. I am a former Army Reservist and have respect for them. But having been one, I can relate and have an understanding of the lack of funds and training that sometimes plagues those branches of the military. I can't help but wonder how some of these units were being used in this theatre. Artillery, maintenance, and even infantry units had been used in the police mission. I really felt some of them were out of their element and had to wonder about the training they had received to prepare for Iraq. Even using Regular Army Infantry units as police trainers was questionable. I'm not impugning their professionalism or commitment, just the decision to send units into an area such as Iraq and for a mission they may not have been up to speed to perform. I have to say at times it seemed to be a numbers crunching game more than anything else.

JUNE

The month of June was hot with the mercury rising to near 120 degrees. I went out on eight missions. Early morning or night was better—at least, it wasn't as hot as the middle of the day. Visiting a police station at night wasn't generally very productive as far as conducting training or accomplishing much else. It amounted to just making sure the station was still there and at least being manned by Iraqi Police officers. Usually only one junior officer was present, and about half of the force on duty was asleep. The militia did a good job keeping the insurgents out of Sadr City; the police had no fear of attack by the militia as long as they hadn't made them mad. Several of our missions were cancelled that month because the MPs were tasked again to other priorities.

On the twenty-fourth, I got to move into the main C.P.A.T.T. barracks with everyone else. Scott had moved a few weeks before, and I was about the only I.P.L.O. in that building. The main barracks was a two-story metal building with concrete barriers around it but no overhead cover. I was on the ground floor, so I figured if we got hit by something, it had to travel through two floors to find me. At least the main barracks had wireless internet. Before, I had to come to the main barracks to get on, or go to one of the internet cafes.

LEAVE

On the twenty-fifth, I took a chopper flight to the BIAP. I spent two nights in a transient tent then flew to Jordan on the twenty-seventh. I stayed at the Sheraton, had a nice steak dinner, and got a nice hot shower and a good night's sleep. I left Amman and flew to Paris on the twenty-eighth. When I changed planes in Paris, I was able to upgrade my ticket to first class for the first time ever. I had always flown coach; first class was nice.

While at home, I celebrated my grandson's second birthday, got a massage and another tattoo (a skull with a helmet and "OIF," Operation Iraqi Freedom), ate out a lot at my favorite places like Outback and Carrabba's, and had a Fourth of July barbeque. I made a point of having at least one night with Bren, went to a cigar bar owned by a friend from my short stint at FCCJ as an instructor, and rode around "topless" in our convertible '04 GT 'Stang. To top off the night, we enjoyed champagne and chocolate covered strawberries. Sorry, but that's it! This isn't that kind of book!

TIME TO GO BACK

I had to go back on the thirteenth, and it seemed to get harder and harder to leave. I could have quit at any time and emailed or called back with an excuse for not returning. My pride wouldn't let me, though. I had to finish what I started. I had a big breakfast of eggs—bacon and all the good stuff. Bren and my son saw me off at the airport. I flew through Frankfurt where I was laid over for about eight hours. Met a guy from Blackwater, and we sat in a restaurant eating and talking for hours. I finally arrived in Jordan about 0200 on the fifteenth. I was able to catch the 1000 flight to Baghdad and a 1700 chopper flight back to Rusty. Mel Lankford was returning from leave and was on the same chopper. That was probably the easiest return trip I had, but I was exhausted.

NEW VEST

When I was home, I ordered a new ballistic vest. I just wasn't happy with the one I was issued. Scott had one he had special ordered and let me try it out, and I really liked it. I spent the first day back getting it together, putting on ammo pouches, and getting it organized. I know I busted on guys before about being "Rambos" with everything in the world hanging off them, but this wasn't that bad. This one just fit better, was much cooler, and was easier to get on and off. It also gave more flexibility as to where I put stuff. I took the trauma plate from my other vest and put it into the new one, too. I spent almost a grand on it, so I hoped it was worth it.

JET LAG

It took me about a week or more to recover from my trip; I had caught a cold in addition to jet lag. Fortunately we didn't have a mission for a few days. Was having a hard time sleeping at night, so I tried to nap in the afternoon. That got interrupted by a mortar attack on the seventeenth. For me, it was always tense going out that first time after leave. I guess you're there physically, but mentally you're still at home to a degree—at least that's how it was for me. My first mission back was on the twentieth of June. We got mortared twice that day, before mission and after we returned to camp. Things were pretty much as I had left them.

JULY

For me July was a long month, trying to rebound from jet lag, a cold, and the fact we only had four missions. It was better to stay busy; slack time gave me the opportunity to think too much. I really tried to stay busy on down days— gym, e-mail, movies, and eating. You got to know what day it was by the menu in the chow hall. For example, Friday night was steak and lobster night, my personal favorite. Sunday was ham, turkey, and roast beef. The dining facility workers did a great job. I was having issues; I didn't feel at this point I was accomplishing as much as I would like. We heard almost daily about soldiers from Rusty or other camps in the area being killed or wounded. I was seriously questioning what was going on. Were we doing the right thing? Were we making a difference? Was I making a difference?

The weather was getting really hot now—130 degrees and higher. It was also hot in other ways; the camp was mortared again on the twenty-fifth and twenty-seventh. On the latter, I was in the gym, and of course everyone drops what they're doing and heads for a bunker. On the thirty-first, I worked out at the "PX Gym." After I was done, I was walking back to the barracks and heard what I thought was a jet going overhead. Mel Lankford lived next door to me and came up to me a little later and said, "It's a good thing you didn't work out today."

I responded, "I did. Why did you say that?"

"Well, the PX Gym got hit by a rocket or mortar round, and several soldiers were wounded." I asked Mel what time this happened, and he told me around 2:30 p.m. Well, I had signed out around 2:28 or thereabouts.

I told Mel, "Man, I had just left there; I thought I heard a jet, but it must have been the round, but I didn't hear the explosion." Mel said something to the effect that I was lucky or fortunate. I told him it was more than luck, and that I thought God was looking out for me.

Now, several soldiers were wounded, and I never knew the exact number. After the incident, I heard conflicting stories as to if any of the wounded had died or how many. Another close call that day was for Chad Hermes. His squad got hit by an IED, and no one was wounded. I went to the gym the next day. It was wrecked. The round had come through the roof making an eight foot hole roughly, apparently showering the room with shrapnel and debris. Rusty was attacked at least five times in July. Except for the wounded in the gym, there were no others. They were bad enough, but it could have been much worse I suppose.

TENSION OVER ISRAEL

August was a tense and uncertain month. Israel had bombed and entered Lebanon to go after Hezbollah. There were pro-Hezbollah demonstrations in Sadr City—all over Iraq, for that matter. Defense Secretary Rumsfeld and Generals Pace and Abazid were appearing before the senate on the conduct of operations in Iraq. The Israelis fought with Hezbollah for weeks, and we all wondered what the outcome would be and if things in Iraq would get worse because of it. We didn't go out again until the sixth of August, and the squad was training a new unit just arriving in country. We went on missions daily through the tenth. It was like that sometimes; nothing for days then *bam, bam, bam!*

SCOTT HAS A RUN IN AT BIAP

On the sixth, Parker returned from leave. He told me he had a run in with a "company" employee named "Mickey." Her job was to pick people up at the airport and take them to the transient tents or to chow—just make sure they got what they needed while waiting for a flight or transport back to their respective duty station. Scott told me she had a serious attitude about doing her job, and they got into an argument. He said she even called the MPs who told her it wasn't their problem basically. I told Scott he should report the incident to our team leader on camp.

TAXI CAB DRIVER

On the eighth, while on station, the squad got a call to respond to an IED attack that had hit an army convoy. When we arrived, the convoy had apparently departed to the nearest aid station because there were wounded. Two civilian vehicles had been hit also. One had minor damage, and the other's driver had been killed. It was a red four-door taxi. It had been struck by the blast and shrapnel on the driver's side. The side and rear windows had been blown out, and the body was peppered by flying metal. Half of the driver's lower face and neck were blown off, and fresh blood was on the front of his dishdasha. His neck must have been broken due to the unnatural angle his head was lying in. Death was obviously instantaneous, because he was still holding a cigarette in his left hand that was lit and smoking.

The I.P.s pulled the man from the car, wrapped him in a sheet, and put him in the bed of their truck to transport to the forensics hospital or morgue. The man was an older gentleman, probably trying to make a few bucks to support his family and happened to be at the wrong place at the wrong time. When we returned, I hit the gym to blow off some steam. The camp got mortared, so I had to hightail it to a bunker.

RUSTY DENTIST

On the tenth, I broke a tooth in half at chow. The next day, I went to dental sick call. The dentist was a guardsman from Pennsylvania; he had a practice back home. He drilled, ground, and filled my tooth with no Novocaine. Hope he did better for his patients back home.

SCOTT GETS FIRED

Scott received word that he had been fired because of the incident with "Mickey" at the BIAP. Didn't take long to decide on that, but that was typical. Scott had a lot of experience—SWAT, paramedic, etc.—and it was going to be wasted. We had heard that several other people had problems with her, too. She must have been somebody's favorite; it seemed that the IPLOs were low men on the totem pole. We were there doing the real mission, but the support people at times were treated better and considered more important; they were actual employees, and we were just contractors, I guess. To me this was a typical example of that. He left on the twelfth. He called me later and told me he'd be in Baghdad for a few days because apparently his incident hadn't really been investigated. He ended up being fired anyway and left country on the twenty-first. He was a great guy and fun to work and hang out with. He went on to be a Federal Agent with the Department of Energy. This meant I'd have to break in a new partner at some point.

PURPLE HEART

On the twelfth, our squad leader received a Purple Heart for being wounded by a roadside bomb. Several months earlier, his squad was on a mission, checkpoint or something like that. He was dismounted from his vehicle and walking on the shoulder of the road when a small device detonated, spraying him with dirt and shrapnel; fortunately his wounds were superficial and was back on duty the next day. It was fortunate he wasn't hurt badly, not necessarily that he returned to duty so soon.

SNAFU

The fourteenth sort of typified how things went sometimes— Murphy's Law, miscommunication, etc. An early morning mission had been scheduled, so I got up around 0500 to get ready and attend briefing. When I reported, there was no activity. The soldiers had to be up early preparing the Humvees and usually had them lined up next to the briefing room. I finally found out the mission had been changed to 1830. When we went outside the wire, the army ran a tight schedule; you were to depart exactly at such and such time, be on station for "x" number of hours, patrol with the I.P.s for a prescribed time, etc. We ended up leaving that night four hours late because of mechanical issues and spent thirty minutes on station—a lot of trouble for nothing—risking the lives of roughly twenty people to accomplish not one thing. It wasn't the squad leader's fault; they had to follow orders and couldn't scrap a mission no matter how useless it might be.

118TH MP CO

The 258th MP was nearing the end of their tour and had been training the 118th MP Co (Airborne) to take its place. I would be assigned to the 2nd platoon, 1st squad under SSG James Jones. On the sixteenth, those of us assigned had a meeting at the 118th to meet our team leaders, get acquainted, and discuss objectives. The squad had a rough start as most did, getting vehicles and equipment squared away, meeting start times, learning the "AO" or area of operation, etc. It took a while to build up a rapport and fit in with the squad. They were all a great group of professional soldiers. It just took them a while to get used to the idea they had a civilian to "babysit," I suppose. Although the 258 was not doing station visits, they were not just sitting around. They still had other missions outside the wire to conduct.

AUGUST

August was miserably hot, reaching up to and over 140 degrees. I felt bad for the soldiers because they had a lot more gear than we did, and they were required more stringently to wear it just about everywhere. Our rules were more relaxed, which I'm sure caused heartburn with some. I had seven missions during August with the 118th. Spent most of the time getting them acquainted with the stations and their commanders. It took some time for them to get their feet wet. Several missions were early morning ones. Usually every morning you could hear explosions in the area and hoped and prayed no one was hurt or killed. I always hated those, I always felt like a guinea pig out looking for the IED's. There were EOD units that were always sweeping the routes for bombs, but they couldn't and didn't sweep every route every single day to my knowledge.

SNIPERS

Statistically, I believe the early convoys got hit more than any other time of the day. Early morning missions always made me more anxious than ones later in the day. Another threat that arose was snipers. From the intelligence given at briefings, they were well equipped with weapons such as Russian-made Dragunov 7.62mm sniper rifles, and that they were possibly trained in Iran. It seemed that they must have been fairly well trained regardless of where they received it, because numerous soldiers were reportedly wounded or killed by sniper fire; two were sniped on the twenty-seventh.

On a couple of missions, we stopped at Camp Shield, which was about five to ten minutes away from Rusty, to eat chow. I hooked up with Mike Alberts and a few others that had been transferred from Rusty to Camp Shield. I also saw Harold Martin; he was one of the "flips" from Kosovo that had gone to Iraq in 2004 with me. He was working for MPRI as an instructor at the Academy. On the twenty-ninth, SSG Jones was tasked to take the squad to Al Quds police station because of possible Mahdi Militia activity. They were directed to look for a weapons cache and illegally held prisoners based on intelligence received. No weapons or prisoners were found; that did not appear to be legitimate.

NEW PARTNER

On the thirtieth, I got a new partner, Mark Williams, from Missouri. Good guy, laid-back, had lots of good police experience, too. Mark and I spent a few days getting to know each other, giving him the scoop on what was going on and what to expect, or not to expect. At this point, I still didn't feel like I was accomplishing much. With everything going on though, I had learned anytime you came back safely, it was a mission accomplished. Mark and his group arrived on the twenty-third of August, and we got mortared the second, fourth, and the sixth of September. At least they got a proper welcome. I spoke to my first squad leader on the eighth of September in the chow hall. He told me one of their squads had been hit the day before. They were on a mission inspecting some I.P. checkpoints and were hit by an IED. A sergeant and a specialist had received minor wounds. I knew both of them and am thankful their injuries weren't serious.

ROCKET ATTACK ON THE 118TH

On the ninth, the camp got hit by several rockets. One of them hit the 118th's barracks around 2100. It came through the roof and wounded seven soldiers. We spoke to SSG Jones; all the guys from his squad were unhurt. We found out around 2240 that one of them had died. He was a young soldier, chilling out on his bunk after a hard day passing the time with his buddies. Maybe they were talking about home or girlfriends or any number of things young American soldiers talk about in their free time. He never saw it coming, wasn't aware of the impending danger, oblivious his young life would soon be over. A memorial was held for him on the fourteenth. After that, another flag-draped casket would be sent home to a grieving family.

LOST RADIO

Fifth anniversary of 9/11. Shortly after exiting the camp gate en route to a station visit, a handheld radio fell off one of the Humvees; someone had left it on top. We stopped, turned around, and dismounted to look for it. This area next to the camp was a trash dump, so that didn't help. It was hot and stunk to high heaven. After looking for thirty minutes or so and being unable to find it, we figured someone had seen it and picked it up. We proceeded to the station and were only on station a few minutes when SSG Jones received orders to return and search for the lost radio. We spent about two hours before permission was given to stop searching. We then proceeded back to Habibya for a visit. It made for a long, hot, and frustrating day.

SEPTEMBER

September was an active and busy month so far and would continue to be so. We did a total of eight station visits and didn't accomplish a great deal in my opinion. On the seventeenth, an IPLO was killed by a sniper in the Tikrit area. Mark had gone through deployment training with him and was pretty upset by the news. On the eighteenth, the 519th MP BN had a "coin" ceremony. They gave us a unit coin with their "viper" logo and a certificate of appreciation for working alongside their soldiers in the police mission.

FIRST IED

The twentieth of September will be one of those days I won't forget, in addition to others past and future. We were traveling on route Pluto, one of the main roads by Rusty used to travel to Sadr City. We were just north of route Aeros, which runs east-west of Pluto. The time was approximately 2215 when my vehicle (211) was rocked by an explosion. I could see the reddish orange blast. Dust and dirt filled the passenger compartment, and I could smell and taste the burnt explosives.

SSG Jones called out, "Is everyone okay?"

Specialist Lee who was the .50 gunner answered, "I'm good, Sarge."

PFC Emery who was driving responded, "I'm okay, Sergeant Jones."

"I'm good, Sarge!" I yelled out.

Then he checked with the other vehicles and determined there were no casualties.

We did a security halt, and SSG Jones called in to the TOC (Tactical Operations Center) back at camp, "IED strike! IED strike! Grid MB 47247 91380, no casualties, over!" He was instructed to remain there and wait for an EOD (Explosives Ordinance Disposal) unit to come and sweep for any possible secondary devices. We waited for about an hour, which made us all uncomfortable—it did me. I kept expecting an RPG (Rocket Propelled Grenade) attack or maybe small arms fire, which would have been typical. The device had been attached to the bottom of a metal foot traffic bridge, which crossed over Pluto. It detonated behind our vehicle and in front of the Humvee behind us.

We finally got the order to proceed to Habibya station. The blast left some minor shrapnel damage to several of the trucks; shrapnel had hit Lee's gun turret. Needless to say, we were all keyed up—at least I was. It was hard to settle down and concentrate on the job. I was thankful everyone was okay and thought to myself, *Well, that's over with, and that wasn't so bad.* I had always been anxious about getting hit, and I figured it was only a matter of time. Each time you left the wire, it was a roll of the dice, so to speak. I firmly believe in God and know he has a plan for us all. Getting hit was a strong possibility for the unfaithful as well as the faithful. That same day two 1st Infantry Division soldiers were killed by a type of IED called an EFP (explosive formed projectile). It was an explosive device with a concave metal disc that turned into a molten projectile that had the capability of punching right through armor plating. Two had died, and we had escaped unscathed. It made me ask, "Why, God?" Why did two young men have to die? What have I done to deserve to live in their place?

CHANGE OF COMMAND

On the twenty-second, the 759th MP BN relieved the 519th in a formal change of command ceremony. The twenty-fourth was the beginning of Ramadan, which is a time of fasting, prayer, and peace for Muslims. A bomb exploded in Sadr City, killing around thirty people—so much for peace and prayer. On this date, we also started going to a new station, Bab Al Sheikh Local Police Station and Bab Al Sheikh HQ. They were in the same building in another area outside Sadr City. The next day, we had a celebration of our own; some of the guys had made arrangements with the chow hall and got the makings for a barbeque. On the twenty-sixth, we went to the camp range. It was always fun. I got to fire different weapons on full automatic. It was a way to release some stress. Two soldiers were wounded during a mortar attack on the twenty-eighth. September was an eventful month. I hoped October would be a little less memorable.

SADR CITY NOT SAFE

On October 12 and 14, our "friend" at Habibya warned us that it was no longer safe for us to come to Sadr City, as if it was so much safer before. The Madhi Militia was being told to become more aggressive with the American forces entering Sadr City. According to him, this was to come in the form of IEDs and ambushes and that Iranian factions were trying to encourage this. I personally took this seriously, because this I.P. had always been frank with us, and most of what he told us was factual. In reality, Sadr City was fairly safe for us; the militia kept out any insurgents, and those that were caught were executed. For all their bad press, they did a good job of keeping the bad guys out of their community. It wasn't subject to the car bombers or suicide bombers as the rest of Baghdad seemed to be—at least not with the same frequency.

GOOD-BYE, SADR CITY

We had stopped going to Al Thawra weeks ago; the last visit I was present for was August 9. They were capable of doing their jobs and were well supplied. We couldn't do anything for them, not that I ever felt we had offered them much to begin with. Scott and I had enjoyed going there because there was a building right next to the station that housed several very poor families. In fact, when you got on the station's roof, you could look over onto the adjacent roof. We brought things to the families when we could. Both our wives sent packages to us, and we gave out toys, clothes, toothpaste, shampoo, etc. We did this at all the stations when we could. Sometimes we would have to stop, because the kids would get overzealous in their attempts to get stuff from us; okay, some of them were downright greedy and would run over the smaller children.

August 17 was the last time we visited Al Nasir. This was due to a lack of cooperation on the station commander's part. We were "punishing" them by not checking on them. I'm sure they were crushed by this. The seventeenth of October was the last time I visited Habibya station. Station visits were stopped in Sadr City for a period but resumed after several weeks. I never returned, because in the interim, Mark and I had been assigned other stations to visit.

SECTARIAN VIOLENCE

I had been to Habibya station over fifty times. Of those visits, I had personally witnessed on a dozen occasions the executed bodies of sectarian violence. It ranged from one to five or six murdered bodies at a time. Each visit we asked the officer in charge to give an update as to major incidents that had occurred, specifically the number of bodies recovered on the days we had not been to the station. It was seldom that they didn't have several to report. Between what I saw in person and the numbers reported to us, it had to be well over one hundred victims. A few were reported to be women, which was somewhat unusual even under the circumstances. I never saw any female victims myself.

Most of the slain were bound with rope and even hand-cuffed, blindfolded, and shot in the back of the head. Some had plastic wrapped around their heads. Others showed bruising and had broken bones from torture. A few had signs of being tormented with a drill—neat round holes in knees, elbows, abdomens, or heads. To add insult to injury, when the bodies were recovered, they were stacked in the back of an I.P. truck like cord wood. Some of it was pretty gruesome.

CIGARETTE FACTORY

There's an old abandoned industrial complex in Sadr City, which used to be a cigarette factory. This is where a majority of the bodies were recovered on just about a daily basis. This is an issue we discussed at nearly every station visit. The number of victims, the frequency of murders, and the fact so many bodies were dumped at the same point would make one think it shouldn't be too hard to catch someone. Well, that wasn't the case. We encouraged and even goaded them to make more of an apparent effort to take action.

IS IT THAT DIFFICULT

As far as I know, the majority of the victims recovered at the cigarette factory were Sunni. Sadr City was for the most part Shia, including the I.P.s. Eventually, a "task force" was supposedly created to address this problem. One of the lieutenants at Habibya was put in charge. It was rumored he was Mahdi Militia, so that's like putting the fox in charge of the hen house. Now, this came from several different sources; no smoking gun, but there seemed to be some veracity to the claim.

It was either that or total incompetence. There never seemed to be any sense of urgency with the I.P.s. Maybe it was the Sunni-Shia issue, or maybe it was that there were so many murders/fatalities daily, they were to the point it wasn't a big deal and were resigned that it was just an unpleasant fact of life. I always made sure to emphasize this aspect in my daily reports, but it never had any impact.

OCTOBER '06

October turned out to be a relatively quiet month for me, which was a relief. On the first, our mission was cancelled. On the second, we got hit by several rockets. C.P.A.T.T. had several SUVs, and I had driven one to the chow hall. When

I came out, there was some commotion going on. I asked a sergeant what was happening, and he told me there was an unexploded rocket in the roadway. Well, it was about fifty feet behind where my vehicle was parked. I asked the sergeant if he thought it was safe to move it. He said, "That's up to you." I told him it was armored, and he responded, "It's your call." I jumped in and got out of there as quickly as I could. On the fourth, we conducted a station visit and nothing out of the ordinary occurred. Our scheduled mission for the fifth was cancelled; SSG Jones was tasked to take the squad out on another mission. On the eighth, there was no water in our shower trailer. The tanks had to be filled periodically, and there was a problem getting that done.

SADR CITY COUNCIL MEETING

On the ninth, Mark and I were asked by a Lt. Mixon of the 118th to attend a council meeting in Sadr City. I had never been, so I thought it might be interesting to attend, and we agreed to go. The meeting was attended by numerous police officials and station commanders, the Mayor of Sadr City and other community leaders, sheiks, etc. One attending official was a U.S. Army Colonel, who I believe was the Deputy Commander of a unit in the 101st Airborne Division. I didn't really understand all that was going on, because I didn't have an interpreter. General issues were discussed, such as security and cooperation between the police, government officials, and our military.

On the tenth, we went out on a mission and stopped at Camp Shield for chow. It's a small world; I bumped into "Doc." He was the Ph.D. developing a literacy test for the

I.Ps, and I worked with him on my first Iraq tour. I also saw Mike Alberts. He told me that a few days earlier he had been sniped. He showed me a burn mark and bruising across his throat. A sniper's bullet grazed him and hit a soldier in the arm that was standing next to him. All I can say is he was fortunate and must have had a guardian angel on his shoulder.

CAMP FALCON

That night after we returned to camp, there were several explosions in the distance around 2230. The next day, the word was that Camp Falcon, which was several miles west of Rusty, had been hit by mortars or rockets. You could see smoke from the direction of Falcon. I also heard that an ammo dump had been hit. I never heard if there were casualties and if so how many. The twelfth was plagued by another vehicle breakdown, delays, and finally a station visit. On Friday the thirteenth, all the I.P.L.O.s were required to attend an intelligence class conducted by a colonel of the 89th MP BDE (Military Police Brigade), if I recall correctly. Someone had developed an elaborate system for the I.Ps to document street contacts, log, collate, and file intelligence information. It was a completely workable system for a police department stateside. All of us in the class agreed that for most of the stations it was a very complicated system that most probably would not understand or use. Those of us working in Sadr City also agreed that this system could work once the militia's influence had been taken out of the equation.

LADY BARBER

On the fifteenth, I went to get a haircut at one of the camp barber shops. The barber I went to was a female; she did a good job, was inexpensive, and spoke English well. She was very friendly, and I enjoyed talking to her. She spoke often of her teenage daughter. It had been several weeks since I had a cut, but her shop was closed. I spoke to some soldiers in a supply room next to the shop; they told me that she had stopped coming to camp because she had received death threats for cutting hair on the camp.

On the seventeenth, we met with the new station commander at Habibya. In our meeting with him, we asked the standard questions about the sectarian violence victims left at the cigarette factory. He said the Mahdi Militia was bad. He also stated he had a plan to catch those responsible, although he wouldn't or couldn't elaborate. Camp Loyalty, which was northeast of Rusty, was hit by mortars, RPGs, and small arms fire resulting in two wounded. Camp Rusty also got hit by a half dozen rockets. Mark and I were eating dinner around 1800 when the rounds started going off. The attack resulted in two possible casualties. Most of the time, the information we got was through the rumor mill, and I never knew most of the time what was true and what was not.

INTEL ON ROCKET ATTACKS

On the eighteenth, we visited Bab Al Sheikh police station. Mark and I were talking to a captain who gave some information about the rocket attacks on Rusty. He stated he thought he knew where one of the launch sites was located. We called in Lt. Mark Singer, the platoon leader, and the captain gave him the information. The launch site was apparently south of the camp in an open field within a residential area. I knew the Lt. would do the right thing and pass the information up the chain of command; I just hoped the powers that be would utilize it. There was a blimp on camp with a radar and/or camera system designed to track where incoming rounds where coming from. There were also mortar tracks (an armored personnel carrier with a mortar mounted inside) set up, but the military was hesitant to return fire, I can only guess, for fear of collateral damage.

We got hit by two rockets around 1900 that night. Mark was driving to the PX and saw one of the rockets hit and told me one soldier had been wounded. While we were on mission that day, workers had turned on a new generator for our building. They apparently crossed some wires or something, because they fried out a lot of people's stuff, including my laptop. At dinner on the nineteenth, I ate with my former squad leader and talked. The 258 was scheduled to leave the thirtieth.

MARK GETS HIT

On the twenty-first, I didn't go out with the squad, because I was going on leave. Mark and the guys left camp around 0800. He called me around 0830 to tell me they were heading back in. I asked him what was up, and he told me they had been hit by an IED, but no one was hurt. The really ironic thing was he had bought a video camera a couple days earlier, was recording, and caught the whole thing. Later he put it to music; AC DC's "Highway to Hell" was the song. Pretty fitting tune, I guess. The Humvee he was in took some minor shrapnel damage, flat tire, cracked windshield, broken headlight, and holes through the "Rhino." Specialist O'Leary was driving, PFC Truelove was gunner and Lt. Singer was the vehicle commander at the time.

The "Rhino" was a metal pole which extended about six feet or so in front of the Humvee with a metal box attached. Inside the box, was a glow plug attached to a power source by a cable that ran the length of the device into the engine compartment.

The idea was the glow plug would generate heat and any IEDs using an infrared trigger system would think the "Rhino" was the engine and detonate, hopefully prematurely, hitting the "Rhino" itself or the engine instead of the passenger compartment. I'm not sure how long it took the bad guys to figure this out, but eventually they would place the devices at an angle to compensate for the length of the "Rhino." To me it was an example of our soldiers ingenuity-not pretty, but cheap, simple and I'm sure it saved some lives.

Another countermeasure used was an electronic system, which was upgraded periodically; it was called a "Duke" or "Warlock." I'm not an electronics guy, and all I know was it sent out radio signals in an attempt to jam any IEDs activated by a pager, cell phone, garage door opener, etc—anything that required some type of electronic signal to work. I think at first, the insurgents used command detonated devices then went to more sophisticated ones, and when we developed countermeasures, they reverted back to the command detonated ones. No way to defeat those for the most part, unless you get lucky and can smoke the trigger man before he does you.

ALL HAD A GOOD TIME

I went down to the 118th's area to check on Mark and everyone when they got back. They were all laughing, joking around, and taking photos, so everyone was fine. I know this is stupid, but I actually felt like I had missed out on something. I heard stories of others who had been in multiple IED hits and had never been hurt. It was like the more you were in, the more bragging rights you earned. Later that day, I flew by helicopter to the BIAP, where I stayed in a transient tent until the twenty-fourth, when I flew to Jordan.

On the twenty-second, Mark called me to tell me one of our guys had been killed by an EFP. He had been at Rusty for two or three months. I didn't know him well but had spoken to him a few times in the hall and had given him a ride to the PX or chow hall. Mark also told me there had been a mortar attack and PFC Denman, who was another soldier in Jones' squad, had been slightly wounded.

FAMILIAR FACES

On the twenty-third, I saw the officer who trained me when I first arrived, and another officer, who I knew from the Basra area and my first Iraq tour. All the Americans had finally been pulled from the Basra area, and they and several others had been living in a tent for two months, waiting for reassignment.

JORDAN

I spent the night of the twenty-fourth at the Intercontinental Hotel in Amman; I had a great dinner there. During dinner I met a very nice Jordanian man who had lived in St. Petersburg, Florida for over a decade many years before. My flight home was typical; the flight from London to Chicago was late, so I missed my flight to Jacksonville. At least they put me up in a hotel overnight for free. Did I mention they lost my luggage? How they can lose a person's luggage so much is beyond me. They must keep track of it, and somehow I was singled out to have mine lost more than the average traveler.

JAMAICA

I arrived in Jacksonville on the twenty-sixth. On the twenty-seventh, my wife and I flew to Jamaica. We stayed at the Sandals resort in Montego Bay—very nice, all-inclusive, all-you-can-eat, etc. I was offered dope—oh, excuse me, I mean ganja—less than five minutes after arriving. When I told the guy I was a cop, he strangely disappeared. The other annoying thing is having guys in canoes come up to you constantly when you're in the water, wanting to sell you trinkets or whatever. I know the economy is bad there, but when you spend the money you do, it's just aggravating. It otherwise was the tropical paradise—sugar white beaches, the water a calm, turquoise color, warm as bath water. Exotic drinks galore made with all manner of tropical fruit—oh yeah—and little umbrellas.

PARADISE LOST

Well, another leave was under the bridge. It had been one of the best I had taken. Bren and I really had some good quality time together, and I knew it was going to be tough saying goodbye. We returned to Jacksonville on the fourth. The next morning, we had a big breakfast, and I said good-bye to the kids. I flew from Jacksonville to Miami to London to Amman. I arrived back in Baghdad the sixth of November and spent several days in a tent, waiting on a flight back to Rusty. I saw my first partner and training officer again; he was ending mission and going home. I wished him well and was thankful he was going home safely. I had a whopper with cheese at the Burger King. I figured it might be the last for a while. I was told that "Mickey" had been fired for mouthing off to one of the "company" bigwigs. But then I heard later she was just moved. Who knows? I arrived back on the tenth.

DANTE'S INFERNO

Everyone was surprised to see me back for some reason—not sure why. It's not like I had a garage sale or anything before I went on leave. On the eleventh, there were a couple of IEDs that detonated not too far outside the main gate. I really had to question how they had been able to plant bombs so close. Was someone asleep? There were guard towers all around the perimeter wall. Later that day, I heard several outgoing rounds from the mortar battery on camp. Not sure if they were illumination rounds or H.E. (high explosive). I hope it was the latter. I heard through the rumor mill they would launch illumination rounds over known launch sites to let the bad guys know that we knew they were there and to "discourage" them from their bad behavior. Killing them would have been the ultimate discouragement in my book. Collateral damage, politics—I can only guess the reasoning. On the twelfth, a 240mm rocket landed near the laundry, but fortunately it failed to explode. There was also another IED attack very near camp. I never heard if there were any casualties. Welcome back to Dante's inferno.

DINNER WITH THE GUYS

That night, Mark and I ate with the squad. We actually ate with them just about every day if possible. We got to be close and respected each other's job. Like I said, we had some SUVs, and we constantly gave the guys rides to the chow hall, PX, etc. They had to wear their gear most of the time, so we tried to make it as easy as we could for them, and they appreciated the gesture. On the thirteenth, I met with Lt. Singer to catch up and update the game plan.

TRAIN AT RUSTY

Although I wouldn't say anything I did was written in stone. I mentioned before it was difficult to set up a firm training plan. Changing schedules, cancelled missions, lack of cooperation, or time on station made it difficult to accomplish much. Also, it was just a bad idea to tell the I.P.s the exact day and time you were going to return for security reasons. Again this was my experience; I'm not speaking for everyone involved. Many of us had suggested we bring the I.P.s to Rusty for training. It would be a relatively secure environment free of distractions with a comfortable classroom setting. Trying to get the upper echelon of the military to buy it proved difficult; it was their house and their rules. There were security issues to consider—planning, coordination, etc. There was also the debate about whether it would take the place of station visits. My thinking was a day or two a month of quality training would outweigh missing a station visit. But the issue was numbers: somebody wanted to see "x" number of visits and "x" number of hours per squad outside the wire. It apparently proved too much, because I never saw it come to fruition.

GOING OUT AGAIN

The fourteenth was our first mission scheduled since I returned but it was cancelled. We went out on the fifteenth. Since this was my first since returning from leave, I was nervous. After going out for a while, I got into a groove, and after leave, it took me a few visits to settle down and get into it again. It was a good, uneventful visit, and I figured at this pace, it'd take us a good ten years to work all this out. On the eighteenth, Mark, Sheldon Ames, and I had lunch at a new café on camp run by some locals. They served hamburgers, fries, or kebabs. It was good—a change of pace and cheap. Sheldon was a retired cop from Pennsylvania in his fifties. A big, strong, barrel-chested guy, he benched well over three hundred pounds. He was also a fine Christian man. He had a son in the Marine Corp who was also serving in Iraq at the time.

Several rockets were launched at the camp, and one or two hit the 118th's motor pool on this day. Fortunately there were no casualties. On the twentieth, a Fox News crew was assigned to us on our visit to interview the soldiers and record the goings-on. Back in May, a CBS News crew was out with an army unit and was hit by a car bomb with several casualties. Some of us weren't crazy about the idea, but it all went over without a hitch. They promised Mark a CD with the whole report, which he never received.

WORD FROM A FRIEND

We were late arriving at Bab Al Sheikh on the twenty-first; we had arranged to train some of the station's investigators, but this got scrapped. By the time we arrived, they had all left or were "busy." Rusty got pounded while we were out, which resulted in several being wounded. On the twenty-second, I spoke to our "friend" from Habibya station. He had given us information on occasion and had warned us to stop coming to Sadr City. He had called me several days before, but under the circumstances, I hadn't answered his call without first getting SSG Jones' approval.

He asked how we were all doing and was glad everyone

was doing well. I asked him how he was doing; I worried that someone might take a disliking to him since he spoke English and conversed with us freely. He had quite a story to tell. He stated several weeks ago he had taken some South African men to Habibya station to protect them from the Mahdi Militia. He relayed that he had called me, but I didn't answer, I informed him I was in the states and to tell me more about what happened. He said after he couldn't reach me to see if we could help, he took the subjects to the MOI (Ministry of Interior) to turn over for their protection. He stated after this, he received death threats from the Militia, and they had ambushed him while he was driving his car and had killed one of his cousins. He said he was in hiding, and his tribe was protecting him. His tribe had told the militia if he was harmed, they would kill any militiaman they caught in public.

I don't have any idea who the South Africans were or how they ended up in Sadr City or what their fate was. I don't know what happened to our "friend." I hope he is well. I reported this to SSG Jones, who passed it up the chain of command. I never received any information back from the military as to any of this.

BIBLE STUDY

Starting on the sixteenth, I attended a Bible study on Thursday nights. Mark Williams, Sheldon Ames, Quinten Warren, I, and on occasion a soldier or two would show up. They were all good people. We had some good discussions about service to God, families, and the possibility of death came up on more than one instance. We had already seen several we knew or knew of that had been killed; it was a definite possibility. Anyone who denied this was fooling himself. It had to make everyone think at least once of their own mortality. I can tell you I prayed daily, especially when we went out on a mission. I have always especially liked the Lord's Prayer and the 23rd Psalm. I repeated them as we were leaving the camp with emphasis on "Yea though I walk through the valley of the shadow of death, I will fear no evil for thou art with me." The time I spent talking with those guys and studying the word of God really lifted my spirit and helped me get through it all.

THANKSGIVING

The twenty-third was Thanksgiving Day, and the chow hall was decked out in the traditional decorations. I made sure I ate a good lunch, because we were going out, and you never knew what might happen. While I was eating, a mortar round landed right outside my room in the barracks. Fortunately the concrete barriers kept anyone from getting hurt inside. Unfortunately, a soldier was standing a short distance away, talking on his cell phone and was wounded. I heard later that he lost an eye. While on station, we heard one or two explosions in the distance. Some of us went on the roof top of the station to see what was happening, all the time being mindful of snipers and trying to keep a low profile. We could see plumes of smoke in the distance and heard several more explosions. The explosions were pretty large, and one can only assume they were car bombs.

UNDER FIRE

On the way back to camp, we linked up with another squad returning—safety in numbers. When we were going through a traffic circle, I heard small arms fire, and one of the .50 caliber gunners in a Humvee ahead of us opened fire. *Bomp, bomp, bomp.* He was shooting at an eight to ten-story building in our front. I never did know exactly what happened—if we had been fired at or if it was random gunfire. Apparently, the machine gunner was convinced enough to shoot back.

On the twenty-fifth, there was violence all over Baghdad, more sectarian violence. Sunnis attacked Shiites, who retaliated in kind. One rocket or mortar hit camp about 2330 that night. There were no casualties that I knew of. We got hit again on the twenty-seventh, while I was in the gym. When you heard the first round hit—*whoomp!*—you kind of hunkered down and waited for the next. If there was one, you scrambled for the nearest bunker. When we visited the station again; it had been hit by an RPG on the twenty-fifth, and it took a small chunk of brick out of the wall and left a scorch mark. There were no casualties among the I.P.s.

UNIFORMS

The next day one of the Staff Sergeants in the 118th gave me a new pair of ACUs (Army Combat Uniform). We were issued khaki 5.11 Tactical Gear shirts and pants; we weren't required to wear a uniform. Although, some I.P.L.O.s wore some type of uniform they had been able to acquire. This and the fact we were allowed to grow a beard or goatee caused some consternation with some of the senior military. It was debated whether we should look like a soldier or look like a civilian—either way, we were targets, and to me it didn't matter whether you had a uniform on or not. But I could see it coming in the near future; we'd possibly be required to conform to military appearance standards.

DECEMBER '06

On the first of December, the 118th had a range day. SSG Jones invited Mark and me to shoot with them. Of course, I accepted; Mark declined, because he was going out on leave the next day and wanted to spend the day packing. The soldiers were qualifying with their SAWs (Squad Automatic Weapons), and they let me fire one, too. I was able to get a few AKs and an H&K MP 5 from our arms room. The soldiers really got a kick out of the AK and MP 5. It was fun stuff like this that really helped build rapport and friendship with the soldiers.

MARK DEBATES COMING BACK

Mark left for leave on the second. Before he left, we had talked about the possibility of him not coming back. He had a tentative job offer and was supposed to have an interview when he got home. He said it was a really good position but would feel guilty about bailing out on me, the mission, etc. I told him not to sweat it, and his first responsibility was to himself and his family, to do what was best for them. I also got a new partner, Brian Rhodenizer, Runa-mucker, Gardenhoser, whatever. Rhodenizer was a former Marine from Virginia. Brian got a proper welcome; we got hit by rockets or mortars that night.

INTERPRETER KILLED

On the third, we had a training meeting with the 118th. The meetings always went well. And we made plans with the best intentions, but things never seemed to turn out like I hoped. Again, there were just so many obstacles that seemed to arise to prevent quality training or most of the time any training at all. On the fourth, one of the L.A.s was killed by a sniper. His name was "Colin"; all the L.A.s had nicknames. I never knew any of their real names, only M2 , Kojak, etc. Most were very protective of their identities and wore masks. They feared for their safety and for that of their families, and for good reasons. I heard of others that had been killed or wounded since I had been at Rusty.

THE HEADLESS HORSEMAN

Brian got a really good indoctrination on the fifth. We went on a visit to Bab Al Sheikh police station. While there an I.A. (Iraqi Army) squad brought in a body. I had seen quite a few at this point, but this one was unusual. The body was decapitated; that in itself didn't surprise me. However, the head had been skinned or something, leaving a bare skull. The I.A. soldiers said they thought it was dipped in acid. Either way, I'm not sure what the meaning or reason of this was. It reminded me of the headless horseman from the movie "Sleepy Hollow."

On the sixth, we got hit by mortars around 1800 during dinner chow and again about 2130. I received a really nice Christmas package from home. It was hard to get into the Christmas spirit under the circumstances; it just didn't seem that too many people were hearing the message of "peace on earth, good will toward men."

On the seventh, Pearl Harbor Day, we got hit pretty well with rockets or mortars. I had seen quite a bit, but nothing compared to what happened sixty-six years ago or what most of our soldiers had experienced in Iraq. On the ninth, we actually did some training while at the station. Brian and I conducted a class on vehicle and person searches. On the tenth, I went back to see if the barber lady had possibly returned. The shop was closed, and I talked to some soldiers nearby. They told me they heard she had been killed—I should say murdered. I can only take what they told me as the truth, because I never heard differently and never saw her again. It fits the whole scenario. We took several rockets that day, too.

PERMISSION TO OPEN FIRE

I had a station visit on the eleventh—nothing out of the ordinary: one murdered body, bound, gagged, and shot, execution style. Around 0800 on the twelfth, we got hit by about a dozen rockets; good way to start the day. Went to the chow hall around 1130 for lunch. When we arrived, it was closed because intelligence had been obtained that a rocket or mortar attack was imminent. I spoke to a 2nd Infantry Division soldier; the 2nd has a large Indian head on their patch, and he told me something about the earlier attack on the camp. He said that a tower guard had seen the insurgent(s) setting up the tube in preparation to fire. According to this soldier, the guard in the tower had requested permission to open fire on the suspected insurgent, but it was denied. I had no idea if this was true or not; I wanted to think it couldn't possibly be, but as crazy as things were there, it was just possible it was true.

We got hit again about 2100. The thirteenth was barracks clean up day, which consisted of sweeping the halls. Around 1315 two rockets came in and hit a building close by ours. Several of us ran over to see if there were any casualties. The building took a direct hit and the rocket tore it up pretty good; no casualties, thank goodness. I heard later that the day before, thirty-four rounds were fired at us. I have no idea how many actually hit within the camp or fell short or overshot us. It's a good thing they weren't very good. It was hit or miss. They couldn't actually target a specific building, not like our guys could. They just launched them, and they hit where they hit.

NOT DURING SHOWER TIME

On the fourteenth, we had a good station visit and were able to do some training. Around 1845 I was in the shower when a couple of rounds hit camp. Nothing like trying to run to a bunker wrapped in a towel—not to mention it had been pretty cold and rainy. It's always good for a laugh from your buddies. There's always one smart aleck who wants to try and pull your towel away. I got another package from Bren; it contained some gifts for SSG Jones and the squad. I handed them out the next day, and the guys seemed to appreciate it. We went out again the fifteenth and the eighteenth. There were several explosions on the sixteenth around 2100 or 2200. I'm not sure what they were.

FINAL ENTRY

During my Kosovo tour, I didn't keep any journal or calendar, I was able to recreate my doings from old memos, operations' orders, plane ticket stubs, pictures, etc. My first tour in Iraq, I kept a calendar on which I jotted things of interest or importance down. My second Iraq tour, I kept a calendar and a daily journal and kept entries in notebooks for every mission I went out on. December 19, 2006 would be my last entry in any journal or notebook. The following is the entry I made in my journal:

> Slept good. Day off. Worked out. Midnight brief. Tried to nap, no dice. It's been too quiet around here for several days. Makes me wonder what the "Haji cong" are up to.

Obviously "Haji cong" is a politically incorrect reference to the insurgents or militia that we used from time to time. In any situation of high stress, humor helps ease the tension and calm the nerves sometimes.

BRIEFING

We had our briefing at 0001; it was typical—vehicle assignments, mission objective, etc. We were to depart camp at 0100 and return at 0800. I was assigned to vehicle 211 with SSG Jones, as I had time after time before. I'm not really superstitious, but we all got into a habit of doing everything the same way. What I mean is, wanting to be assigned in the same vehicle, sitting in the same seat, wearing your gear the exact same way, etc. Outside the wire, you had to travel different routes to avoid predictability, but everything else you did the same way out of habit or maybe it was superstition. I always sat behind the driver; I had gotten into that habit, because the left rear passenger seat had more legroom. I'm over six feet tall and needed all I could get.

STATION VISIT

We arrived at the station at 0230. There were fifty-five officers and men on duty—or at the station at least. Twelve were assigned to force protection (guard) duty. There were seventeen detainees in the detention cell. Everything was pretty quiet at the station, and at 0315 we left for a joint vehicle patrol with the I.P.s. They had two vehicles with approximately four men each. The convoy was two Humvees, followed by an I.P. truck, followed by my vehicle, another I.P. truck, and finally the fourth Humvee of the squad. We patrolled for about a half hour then we stopped to do a vehicle checkpoint. We dismounted for maybe a half hour or so and checked a few cars. We mounted up and patrolled for maybe another half hour. Then we stopped again to set up another checkpoint. We stayed on the checkpoint until around 0445. SSG Jones decided we'd head back to the station until 0600, and then we'd go get some chow at another camp then head back to Rusty. Sounded good to me.

As we were heading back to Bab Al Sheikh station, it was quiet and we were either talking or absorbed in our own thoughts. SSG Jones was in the front passenger seat, PFC Denman was driving, PFC Lee was the .50 cal. gunner, and as I said, I was sitting behind the driver.

MY LIFE IS CHANGED

Most of the time the gunners tried to keep a low profile to avoid sniper fire. If necessary, they would expose themselves to man the gun or whatever. Lee was hunched down and sitting on the sling seat talking to me. At this time, I can't remember what we were talking about—just small talk I guess. As we drove along Route Grizzlies, I remember looking out the right passenger window and seeing a concrete block wall. Lee partially obstructed my view and I had to lean back to look.

They say your life can change in an instant; well, mine changed in a brilliant, almost blinding flash of orange and red fire. The sound was almost deafening. I remember thinking, "that was a big one." Then I realized we had been hit.

Smoke and dust filled the vehicle; the smell and taste of the explosives filled my nose and mouth. The vehicle stalled from the concussion, and it took a few seconds to clear the "cobwebs" from my mind. Everyone else was quiet for a brief moment. Again it sunk in that we had hit a large device; I remember thinking, *Well, Lord I'm still alive*, and I must have been, because I was still thinking anyway. Finally SSG Jones called out, "Is everyone all right?" Then I did a quick check—had both arms, legs, and could still see, so I guess I was okay. Then I realized I couldn't move my right arm. I wasn't feeling any pain, but it wasn't working. I also realized something was wrong with my face; I could feel the warmth of my blood flowing, even though I had gloves on. Then I started to get a little worried. I thought my face may have been seriously messed up—not that I was particularly good looking before. I felt my face, and as far as I could tell it seemed normal.

I THINK I'M HIT

SSG Jones asked again if everyone was all right. Denman and Lee said they were okay. SSG Jones called out, "Ron, are you okay?" I still wasn't feeling any pain, but I knew I was hurt.

I told Lee, "I think I'm hit."

Lee yelled out, "Sarge, Ron thinks he's hit!"

"How bad?" Jones asked.

I told Lee, "I'm not sure, but I think it's pretty bad." Lee then repeated what I said. SSG Jones asked me if I could get out of the vehicle. I told him I would try and was able to open the Humvee door, which is difficult sometimes even with two good arms.

DON'T PASS OUT, BRO

I managed to walk behind the vehicle, feeling weak and somewhat dazed. Sgt. Matt Thompson, one of the team leaders, came around to check on me. I went to my knees and hung my head down. The blood really seemed to be flowing now. Thompson told me to lie down; I told him, "No." I wanted to stay how I was. I was afraid if I laid down, I'd pass out or drown in my own blood. I kept telling myself, "Whatever you do, don't pass out. Stay in control."

Thompson started taking my vest off and reassuring me

I was going to be okay, that it wasn't too bad. He wrapped me in a field dressing and put me in a Humvee from another squad when they arrived. By this time, I was starting to feel real pain. I don't remember what squad it was that transported me to the aid station at either Shield or Loyalty. I just remember them putting me in the back seat and throwing a vest over me. I was really feeling vulnerable now; not very capable of defending myself and thinking if we get hit, I'm really finished. There were two I.P. (Iraqi Police) vehicles in the convoy, one in front and one behind us that didn't get a scratch. Not saying they had anything to do with it—they had no idea what our patrol route would be—but it is just amazing how we got nailed right in between the two.

AID STATION

It took maybe ten or fifteen minutes to reach the aid station. It seemed much longer. I was repeating the 23rd Psalm and the Lord's prayer over and over in my mind to try to maintain consciousness and my composure. I'd been a John Wayne fan all my life, and it was ingrained that "tough guys" don't cry out. I'd also heard about real-life stories of wounded guys screaming and crying in agony. I wasn't a tough guy by any means; I just wanted to acquit myself well and not be an embarrassment to myself.

We finally arrived at the aid station after hitting every pot hole and jumping over every curb in Baghdad. I was rushed inside, and the medics started cutting and ripping everything I had on off. I had just bought a pair of under armor thermals and was wearing them for the first time and thought, *Well, that figures.*

CAT SCAN

I was taken in for a CAT scan, and the technician was a civilian. So far everyone had been telling me I was fine, no big deal, etc. Well, this guy looks at me and says, "Oh my God!"

I looked at him and said, "You must have failed first aid." The first thing you learn is to reassure the victim. I learned my right arm, shoulder, back, and face got fairly chewed up. There was a hole in my back the size of a fist. I had some visitors, a couple of the C.P.A.T.T. bigwigs, Frank Knight, my team leader, Doug Nichols, and some of the other I.P.L.O.'s from Rusty as well. At some point, I asked if anyone else had been wounded. I was told Jones was fine and that Lee and Denman had gotten minor wounds and were good to go. I was relieved to hear that.

CALLING HOME

I was told I would be flown to the C.A.S.H. (Combat Army Surgical Hospital) in the Green Zone for further treatment. I wanted to know if anyone had contacted my wife Brenda. I knew if someone called and told her I was hurt, she'd freak. I had to call her myself; if I did, it wouldn't be quite as bad on her—at least I hoped. When I finally called her, the first thing I said was "I'm all right, but..." I told her that I was hurt but doing fine. Well, of course she started crying and was upset. I tried to convince her if I was talking to her, it couldn't be that bad. I told her I was fine and that I'd be going to Germany for further care. I can only imagine the agony she and my kids went through after our initial conversation.

GREEN ZONE

I was flown in a medivac chopper to the Green Zone. I don't remember exactly when, but at some point at the aid station, they gave me morphine, because things started getting hazy. At the C.A.S.H., they cleaned and dressed my wound, and from there I was flown to the Army hospital in Balad. In Balad I laid on a cot until the twenty-first, because there was an unusual blanket of fog over the air strip, restricting flights out. I thought that was rather inconvenient. I don't remember too much of the flight to Landstuhl, Germany; I was in and out of consciousness. I do remember noticing that many of the soldiers on the plane were apparently very seriously wounded and missing limbs. I thought to myself that whatever was wrong with me didn't compare to them. I do specifically remember a seriously wounded soldier on the rack below me; his brother was on the flight, holding his hand and comforting him. I also remember being excruciatingly thirsty at this point and how difficult it was to try to drink.

LANDSTUHL

It took several hours to reach Germany; fortunately I was asleep or unconscious for most of it. By the time we landed, I was feeling pretty bad, and again my wounds were nothing compared to most. I can't say enough about the care I got while at Landstuhl. Even though I was a civilian contractor, I was treated no differently. I was given the same consideration and respect as the soldiers. It's not that the staff would have done this, I just didn't know what to expect and feared the worst. I had a total of four surgeries; two on the right side of my face to remove shrapnel from my sinus cavity and to repair a broken cheek and lower eye socket with a metal plate. Two more were performed to remove shrapnel from my right arm, shoulder and back. I had lost a large chunk of tissue from my upper back. Part of my right triceps muscle was detached, and I had a fractured shoulder blade. The doctor removed a large piece of brass or copper, weighing six or maybe eight ounces from my back. When I saw it, I knew we had been hit by an EFP. I kept all the shrapnel as a "souvenir." I was only in the hospital for four or five days, and it seemed I was either going into or coming out of surgery. I was miserable, I was in pain, even though I was on morphine, and I was so dehydrated I was begging for water.

All the doctors and nurses were great; there was one nurse who was really good but tough. She didn't babysit me. She had me up and out of bed going to the bathroom and showering on my own. I got to call Bren a few times to let her know I was doing well. It was a possibility she was going to come and see me, but the doctors could never decide how long I would be there. It wasn't decided until just the day before or even the day of when I was leaving for home.

All things considered, Christmas day was good. It was very heartwarming to be visited by so many complete strangers bearing gifts for all the wounded, again not caring whether you were military or civilian.

There was even a Sergeant Major from the 1st Armored Division making the rounds. We started talking, and he asked me what happened. In our conversation, I told him I had been in the 1st A.D. also. He had been stationed with the 1/1 Cav at O'Brien Barracks outside Nuremburg in the late 70s early

80s. I had been there in '83 and '84. He gave me a nice 1ˢᵗ A.D., "Old Ironsides" coin. I considered it quite an honor and nice gesture on his part. Probably the most uplifting was the several chaplains that prayed with me. Although I am not Catholic, one gave me a Rosary which I have to this day.

LEAVING GERMANY

I left on the twenty-sixth of December. A "company" rep had visited me and made arrangements for my flight home. I was wondering about being ready to travel but was anxious to get home. The rep drove me to the airport, saw me to my plane, and basically said, "Have a nice flight and good luck." I was in pretty bad pain, feeling weak and unsure on my feet. It was a long and miserable time; fortunately the airline was aware of my situation, and the flight attendants did all they could to make it easier for me. Figures the second time I ever flew first class, and I was in no condition to enjoy it.

FINALLY HOME

I arrived home the night of the twenty-sixth. I don't know how I looked, but I know how I felt: rode hard and put away wet. I was pleasantly surprised to see so many of my family and friends gathered to see me home. It made me feel a little better anyway. Bren had been told what to do when I returned home. It was up to us to find doctors to continue my care. After being home for a good week, we were not having any success finding any; my own family doctor didn't want to see me, because I had been hurt overseas. I'd been operated on and was a worker's compensation case. I was in a lot of pain and weak, so just getting up and out of bed or walking up or down the stairs was tough for several weeks.

A DOCTOR AT LAST

Bren finally got me an appointment with a critical care center. The doctor redressed my wounds, gave me some more pain meds, and referred me to an orthopedic surgeon. The insurance company providing the worker's compensation benefits also assigned a case worker. I saw the ortho once before I developed a serious problem. My right arm started to swell up like a balloon, became tight, and was really painful. I ended up in the emergency room where they did a CAT scan. I had developed a serious deep vein thrombosis, or in layman's terms, a blood clot. I spent a week in the hospital getting pumped full of antibiotics and blood thinners. They had to install a pic line, a catheter through my left arm into my chest to accommodate the high volume of fluids. That was fun. I had to stay on blood thinners for six months. The blood clot also delayed my being able to start physical therapy by several weeks. While I was in the hospital, the movement control team leader from my first Iraq tour came to visit me. He lost a leg in September '05 after I left Iraq the first time. He had a prosthetic leg and been through numerous surgeries and months of therapy. He had a great attitude, and he gave me a great deal of encouragement. He made me look at myself and think, "You've got no problems."

RECOVERY

First of all, I want to say I am thankful to God I survived and had all my limbs, eyes, etc. I was much more fortunate than many others returning from Iraq. I went through about ten months of physical therapy but will never have full use of my right arm and shoulder. The blood clot also caused the loss of some use and strength in my right hand. The inability to use my arm and shoulder caused the muscles tissue to atrophy and the shoulder joint to "freeze up." That and the fact I lost a fair chunk of muscle tissue from my back limited my recovery potential. I had another surgery where the ortho "scoped" my shoulder and performed a manipulation therapy; that's where they force the limb to move to tear and break up the scar tissue. Fortunately I was asleep for this. Unfortunately, it wasn't very successful. Overall, I was fortunate and blessed; it could have been much, much worse.

Therapy was tough and painful, but it took me from the point of not being able to use my arm or shoulder to having the ability to do many normal daily functions. All my therapists were great and made me work hard. I have a better understanding and respect now for what they do for people. I have nerve damage in my face, causing numbness and less than full function. A maxi-facial specialist also did a procedure to try and correct some of the damage done to my sinus cavity by the shrapnel; this wasn't too successful either.

I am thankful for my wife, daughter, son, family, friends, and healthcare workers who helped me through it and stood by me. I am especially thankful for my Bren; her love, patience, understanding, and support was so vital to my recovery.

Now, like I said, my wounds weren't life threatening, and I didn't lose a limb. I have even been told on a couple of occasions by people that it was no big deal, that my wounds were nothing. Maybe not in the larger scheme of things, but there were still days of great pain, disappointment, and frustration. The "company" also sponsored an alumni conference where I met some other guys that had been wounded in Iraq, and through some of them, I got a great deal of support and information.

In November of 2007, the doctor released me to go back to work with limitations. He told me I'd probably never be able to return to normal police work or overseas work. When I wrote this, I was looking for a job and trying to collect on a disability insurance policy provided for all the employees working in Iraq. I'm sympathetic to anyone who's been hurt at work and tried to collect; it's tough.

I started writing this as a journal for my kids, grandkids, and family. I hope it turned out to be more than that. This is a story of one guy's experiences in a place that conjures up much controversy and difference of opinion today and probably for a long time to come. I will never forget my experiences—the good and the bad. I had the honor and privilege of working with some great people, military and civilian. I also had the misfortune of working with some officers who weren't so great. I'm sure there are some who would say the same of me. But I can honestly say I tried my best to do the job and hopefully make a positive impression and most importantly make a difference. All who went are in an elite class of men and women that can say with pride we were there and were part of something important. I hope and pray our efforts in Iraq will be successful, and it will probably take years to see it to that end. But whether it is or not, a debt of gratitude is owed to those who have served, bled, and died, whether they were military or civilian.